AND THAT'S DINNER!

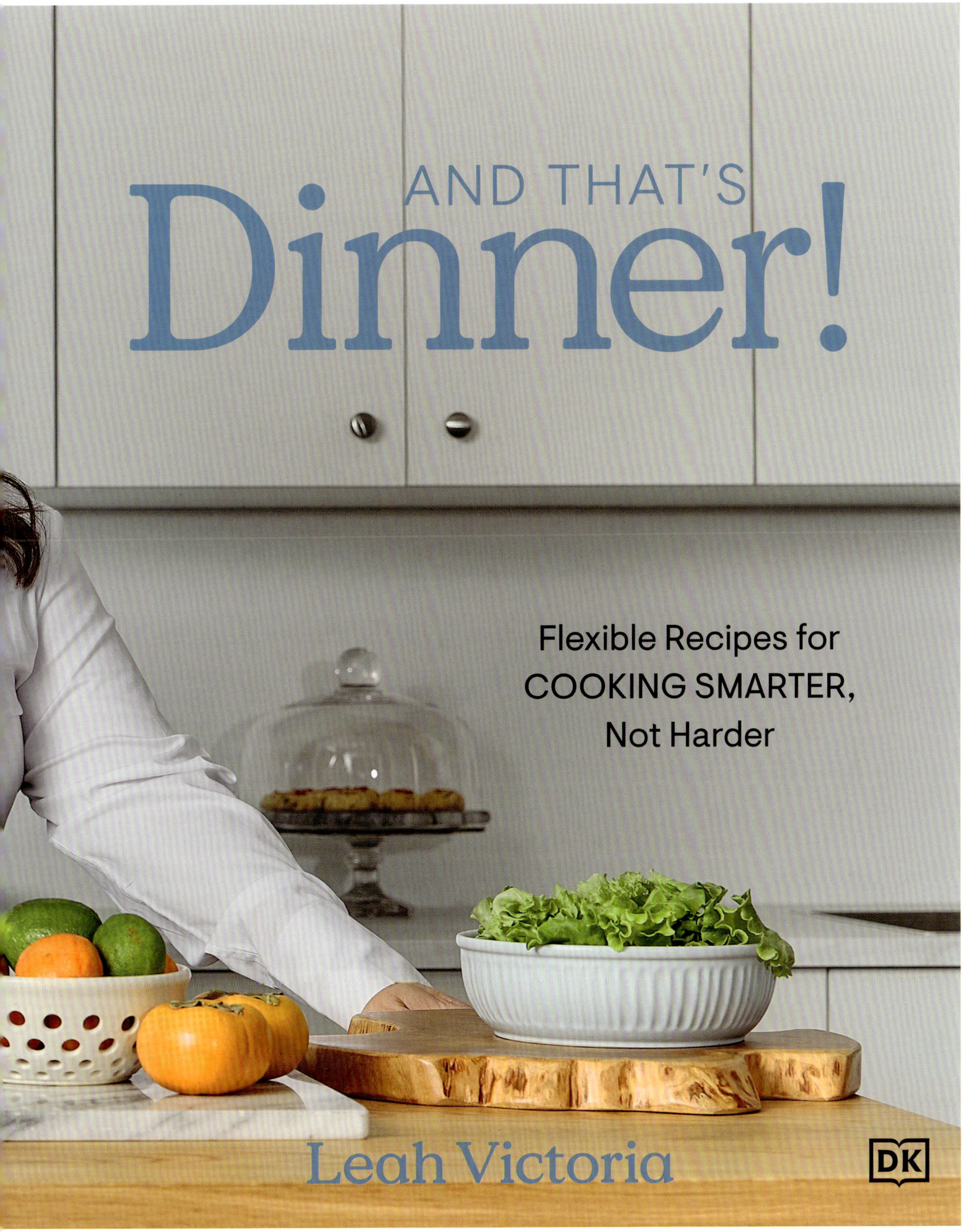

AND THAT'S Dinner!

Flexible Recipes for COOKING SMARTER, Not Harder

Leah Victoria

DK

DK | Penguin Random House

Publisher Mike Sanders
Art & Design Director William Thomas
Editorial Director Ann Barton
Editor Brandon Buechley
Acquisitions Editor Molly Ahuja
Developmental Editor Kelly Vaughan
Cover & Interior Designer Laura Palese
Food Photography Team Robin Chase & Susan von Brachel
Lifestyle Photographer Lee Seidenberg
Recipe Tester Melissa Schwimmer
Copy Editor Mira S. Park
Proofreaders Anna Wostenberg & Lisa Himes
Indexer Beverlee Day

First American Edition, 2026

Published in the United States by DK Publishing
1745 Broadway, 20th Floor, New York, NY 10019

The authorized representative in the EEA is Dorling Kindersley Verlag GmbH.
Arnulfstr. 124, 80636 Munich, Germany

26 27 28 29 10 9 8 7 6 5 4 3 2 1
001-349957-OCT2026

A catalog record for this book is available from the Library of Congress.
ISBN 978-0-5939-6984-7

Printed and bound in China

www.dk.com

FSC www.fsc.org MIX Paper FSC™ C018179

For my two beautiful daughters, my husband, my mother, and my mother-in-law—this one is for you!

Contents

Mains

Appetizers

Pasta

Sides

Cocktails

Baked Goods

(Mostly) Meatless Meal Prep At Work

Chicken Meal Prep At Work

Beef Meal Prep At Work

AND

Welcome!

I guess here is where I should tell you a little about my life and all the things that got us to this exact point. My name is Leah, and I grew up in Howard Beach, Queens, New York. Growing up in an Italian-American household, it is in my genes to cook. I don't remember a whole lot from my childhood but what I do remember is all of us in the kitchen during holidays, laughing at God knows what. Everything revolved around food. Happy times, sad times—it didn't matter! Who is coming and what are you bringing?

My dad left when I was very little, so my mom was a single parent. I always said my grandma was my dad, being there for all the things he was not. This made me and my sister naturally fend for ourselves a lot. I remember being very little, throwing concoctions together in the kitchen, so excited to serve a home-cooked meal to my family. Being in the kitchen brought me so much peace and comfort amongst the chaos. This is where my love of cooking started to evolve.

When it was time for me to go off to college, coming from a traditional household, my mother didn't want me to follow my passion to culinary school. She insisted I went to a "real college," CitiTech in Brooklyn. Of course, I never graduated, dropping out of my program six months in because it was not what I wanted to do. I wanted to work in the food industry. With that, I took my butt on the A train all the way to Canal Street, walked over to Little Italy in Manhattan, and got myself a job in a restaurant. One thing my mother did right was raise a hustler. We didn't grow up with money, so as soon as I was old enough to get a job, I did.

I worked at that Little Italy restaurant for years until I started Leah's Italian Apples, my catering company specializing in rice balls, both savory and sweet. I started building my following and a footprint for myself online. I would sell at local craft markets in churches and breweries all over Queens. It all started at the Feast of San Gennaro. I made 100 rice balls, wrapped them up individually, and stapled my business cards on them. My husband Tom (boyfriend at the time) and I went to Mulberry Street and handed out all these rice balls for free! The only condition was to shout me out on social media. I knew I had a great product; I just needed to get it in the right hands. From there, I was catering weddings, showers, and birthdays. We eventually changed the name to Leah's Cucina to let people know we weren't limited to only rice balls and could cater a much more expansive menu.

Over the years, things got more expensive and the small business was becoming too much for me to handle. I still loved to cook but my vibes were changing. I didn't want to be providing a service anymore—I wanted to teach. I started to transform my catering page to a cooking blog. I would post (and still do!) super detailed tutorials teaching people like you and me about all things cooking. I always reminded them to have fun in the kitchen, be creative, and don't overthink it.

Now look at me, two kids later, twelve years married, in my mid-thirties, and writing my first cookbook—a dream that never seemed attainable for me as a child. All those years of hard work brought me here with this beautiful community that we created. This is all proof that there are bigger plans for you somewhere. You just need to believe in them to achieve them. I am so happy you are here and I can't wait to see all your delicious creations. Thank you; you are appreciated!

Pantry Staples

When it comes to cooking, the pantry is more than just a storage space—it's the mecca of your kitchen. It's no secret that a well-stocked pantry can save you time, stress, and multiple runs to the grocery store. But building a functional pantry isn't about buying every "must-have" on a list or letting ingredients collect dust after one recipe. It's about stocking intentionally and learning, over time, which ingredients actually support your cooking style, your schedule, and your family's vibe. This will vary from household to household, so like I always say, alter these things to your taste buds.

This does not mean run to the store and buy everything to fill your shelves. You accumulate stuff over time. Just start with the basics you know you'll actually use—pasta, rice, a few cans of beans—and build from there. Over time, as you cook more and figure out what your family loves and what you keep reaching for, your pantry becomes less of just a shelf of stuff and more of a secret weapon.

The goal isn't to buy ingredients you'll use once and never again. It's to have things on hand that work for you—ingredients that help you throw together dinner when you're out of fresh groceries, stretch leftovers into something new, or pull off a meal without overthinking it. Eventually, you'll stop feeling like you need a recipe every time you cook and start cooking with confidence just based on what's in front of you.

So, with that in mind, here's a list of pantry staples that can set you up for success and a handful of uses for each.

Grains and Pasta

These are probably my top pantry staples. They can serve as a base for stir-fries, a bed for all kinds of sauces, curries, stews, chilled pasta salads, rice balls—I mean, I could be here all day. Literally anything you want to bulk up and stretch, here you go.

Canned and Jarred Goods

Think beans, veggies, fruits, coconut milk, jarred marinara. These can be added to all sorts of recipes, savory or sweet. The beans can be added to make that dinner meatless, canned fruit for a nice cobbler, canned string beans for an easy side dish, coconut milk to add creaminess to curries, and yes, in my opinion, everyone should keep one jar of good quality marinara.

Oil and Vinegars

I like to keep a nice selection of each. But in the beginning, you should start small. You want a full-bodied extra-virgin olive oil for dressings and drizzling, a lighter olive oil for your everyday cooking, and a neutral oil for cooking at a higher temperature and frying; I prefer avocado oil for this.

Every kitchen needs balsamic vinegar, red wine vinegar, and apple cider vinegar. These will add brightness to your dressings, sauces, marinades, and even in soups and stews.

Baking Basics

Necessities in your kitchen for baking savory and sweet, or even just cooking in general, are all-purpose flour, sugar, honey, maple syrup, baking powder, and baking soda. Having cornstarch on hand will help thicken baked goods, as well.

Canned Chicken and Fish

These belong in your pantry because they have a long shelf life, no prep, and no fuss. The canned chicken can be used in a salad, among many other things. If you're feeling particularly adventurous, you can even use it to create a protein-packed pizza crust. The canned fish alone is high in protein and omega-3s and is such an easy way to add a nutritious punch to meals. I love eating it plain on top of crackers, or even in a quick pasta dish with a spicy marinara. Like I always say, think outside of the box with your ingredients.

Umami

Umami makes food taste more layered and flavorful. It just makes the dish feel more complete with that salty, savory touch. You can find umami in soy sauce, tomato paste, anchovy paste, miso paste, even Parmesan rind. Ingredients like these add a rich backbone to your dish that will have people wondering how you brought out the flavors. It works best when it's balanced with a little bit of acid from some fresh lemon or vinegar, so keep that in mind when you're testing in the kitchen.

Spices and Seasonings

Of course, the nonnegotiables are salt and black pepper. And although I maintain a stocked spice shelf, you won't often see me using dried spices. I prefer fresh flavors over dried, but in some instances, you need the latter. I always have garlic powder, onion powder, smoked paprika, Italian seasoning, curry powder, cinnamon, nutmeg, and, of course, crushed red pepper on hand.

Breadcrumbs

I always have breadcrumbs on hand for coating protein, adding texture to pasta, or even using as a binder. A breadcrumb coating is an easy way to turn a basic dinner into something crispy and golden. They even freeze well, so if you buy a container and you don't see yourself using them, pop them in a zip-top bag. Make sure you add a date on it and freeze it up to three months.

When your pantry is stocked with purpose, cooking feels way less overwhelming. You're not reinventing the wheel every night—you're just grabbing a few building blocks and trusting that you've got what you need to make something work. And honestly, that's a huge win. It gives you flexibility and confidence. Let your pantry grow with you and take note of what disappears fast. Eventually, you'll look around and realize you have your own list of staples and they might even look different than mine.

Freezer Staples

Having a freezer stocked with versatile staples is like giving yourself a helping hand in the kitchen. In fact, your future self will thank you. Whether it's precooked grains that cut your dinner prep time in half, frozen herbs that bring dishes to life, or leftovers ready to rescue you on a busy night, having frozen shortcuts on hand takes the pressure off and keeps meals feeling fresh and easy. It's not just about convenience—it's about making home cooking more doable, more flexible, and a lot less stressful. Cooking shouldn't be a dreaded chore every night. With the right freezer staples on hand, you're always just a few steps away from a delicious, homemade meal, no matter how hectic the day gets.

The following is a curated list of my favorite freezer staples that I use in my everyday cooking. This list is designed to guide you in stocking your freezer efficiently and making the most of what you have, whether it's for quick weeknight dinners, meal prepping, or enhancing your skill in the kitchen. Keep these basics on hand and you'll always be ready to cook up something tasty without the hassle.

Frozen Vegetables

- Frozen veggies are great because they are frozen at peak ripeness, they retain nutrients and flavor longer than fresh veggies that spoil quickly, and they are so convenient for quick meals.

- Use them in stir-fries, soups, casseroles, pasta sauces, smoothies (spinach or kale shine here!), or even just as a side dish.

Frozen Fruits

- Just like frozen veggies, frozen fruit is great for so many things. It is available all year-round, perfect for smoothies or baking, and there's no worry about spoilage. Plus, you can usually find even the off-season fruits that you won't be able to find fresh at certain times of the year.

- Use frozen fruit in smoothies and desserts (crumbles, pies, cobblers, trifles) but also for breakfast as toppings on yogurt or oatmeal. Or how about a homemade jam? Or even, my favorite, in a nice cocktail.

Frozen Meat and Poultry

- Freezing extends the shelf life of meat and poultry significantly. I like to keep ground beef, ground turkey, chicken breast, and bacon on hand.

- Defrost frozen meat and poultry as needed for roasts, stews, stir-fries, BBQ, tacos, and soups.

Frozen Doughs and Bread

- Frozen doughs like pie crust and puff pastry are handy to keep in the freezer for quick meals—as are loaves of sliced bread. Pick up an extra loaf when bread is on sale and stash it in the freezer.

- Sliced bread toasts up beautifully from frozen—you wouldn't even know the difference. Use it for sandwiches, toast, stuffing, and breadcrumbs (toast, then crumble). Frozen pie crust and puff pastry dough give you savory or sweet options. Make a nice quiche or even a cherry pie.

Frozen Herbs

- If you have a bunch of fresh herbs and you aren't able to use them in time, freeze them! Freezing is great way to use up those herbs in your garden. The more you prune those plants, the more abundant your harvest will be. To freeze, wash and chop fresh herbs. Add the chopped herbs to an ice cube tray with olive oil (to prevent freezer burn) and freeze.

- Cubes of frozen herbs can be added directly to cooked dishes, marinades, dressings, dips, and spreads for fresh flavor.

Frozen Broth and Stock

- Broth and stock are the secrets behind making soups, sauces, and even rice taste like it's been cooking all day. They add a lot of flavor quickly and easily. Freezing them in ice cube trays or even portion size zip-top bags allows you to always have the right amount, rather than having to freeze and thaw a big batch.

- Broth or stock (because I use them interchangeably) can be used in so many things! A few would be soups, stews, braised dishes, poaching, sautéing, deglazing, or even simply as the cooking liquid for grains.

Frozen Precooked Grains and Legumes

- Precooking your grains saves so much time when creating your meals. I freeze cooked grains like rice, couscous, lentils, barley, and more.

- Frozen cooked grains just have to be reheated and they're ready to use. Most grains maintain their texture well, and I love to add them to stews, soups, and even chilled salads for added fiber and protein.

Tips for Freezer Success

Purchase in Bulk

When it is feasible, don't pass up on buying meats and poultry in bulk. Buying larger quantities reduces the cost per pound and allows you to have a well-stocked freezer, which makes meal prep more convenient. When you get home from the grocery store, immediately break down large packages into smaller portions for freezing. I freeze everything roughly in 1-pound portions. You can use a food saver if you have one, but honestly zip-top bags work just fine. Press all the air out of the bag and try to lay them as flat as possible for easy stacking in the freezer. The first step is being prepared and that's exactly what this is—this helps take a lot of the guesswork out when dinnertime rolls around.

Prep Precooked Proteins

Precooked proteins make easy grab-and-go meals. Here are some options that I know freeze well:

- Cooked shredded chicken. You can use this in so many ways. Build a big salad or make sandwiches, wraps, tacos, quesadillas—the list goes on.
- Baked or fried meatballs made from ground beef, turkey, or chicken. You can throw together a dinner quickly with these—whether you decide to do meatball parm, meatball stew, or even a nice pizza with a meatball topping.
- Muffin-tin meatloaf. I love making meatloaf in muffin tins—more surface for texture. Prep and bake as usual, then freeze. When ready to serve, take them out of the freezer, brush the tops with a little barbeque sauce, and pop back in the oven at 350°F (180°C) for 10 minutes just to warm them through. All you need to do is make a side. Everyone can use something comforting on a busy weeknight.
- Cooked and seasoned ground meat—this could be beef, chicken, turkey, or even tofu crumbles. Seasoned ground meat opens up so many options for easy weeknight meals. Think chili, burritos, pasta dish, or even a casserole.

Make Extra Soup and Sauce

Soups are the ultimate freezer staple, so make a double batch and stash some in the freezer. Freeze larger portions for a freezer-to-stovetop dinner or in single-serving containers for a great quick lunch—healthy and homemade, how can you beat it? And don't forget that most sauces are freezable too. I remember my mom making marinara sauce on Sundays. She would freeze it and use it weeks later to make baked ziti. I use it to make eggs in purgatory, which is an easy weeknight meal—just eggs poached in leftover sauce. Pesto freezes nicely too, and it's a great way to preserve all your garden basil.

Freeze Your Leftovers

Freezing meals or leftovers is an obvious way to reduce food waste and save time on busy days. You might not want those leftover meatballs tomorrow, but you will want them a month from now when you're scrambling on a Wednesday and it's dinnertime already and you need an easy delicious dinner, quick. Pop those leftovers in the freezer and let them come to the rescue when you need it most. You can warm them up and enjoy as is or repurpose them for something totally new. Lucky for you, I added some repurposed recipes to this book to get you familiar with refreshing those leftovers, like my Meatball and Vegetable Stew on page 45.

Repurposing Tips

Repurposing in the kitchen is important for so many reasons—it saves money, helps reduce waste, and encourages creativity (my favorite reason). The following tips help me thrive in my kitchen on the daily. I hope they help you, too.

1. **If I can teach you anything in this life, it would be to save your veggie scraps.** You can create such a rich and healthy stock from stuff that you would literally be throwing in the garbage otherwise. Homemade stock—whether it's vegetable- or meat-based—supports healthy digestion, boosts immunity, and is great for joint health. I keep a plastic zip-top bag in my freezer full of vegetable scraps from the week. Mostly carrots, onions, garlic skins, celery leaves, herbs—all things that would go great in a chicken soup! Use common sense here. I don't think pepper scraps or mushroom scraps work well, for example. I keep chicken or beef bones in a separate bag. Start with a stock pot and add in the frozen scraps and bones (you can add a combination of both, or keep them separate), cover with water, and season with salt and a splash of vinegar to help bring out the nutrients in the bones and the vegetables. Bring the heat up to a simmer and cook low and slow for hours. Strain out the solids, and you're left with a beautiful stock to create soups, stews, and flavorful braises. You can also freeze in 1-cup portions to add to future recipes. A lot of recipes call for a splash of stock here and there.

2. **I really try my best to utilize the "first in, first out" method.** When you come home with your grocery haul, move everything that you already have in the pantry to the front and put all your newly purchased items in the back. Plan your meals for the next few days based on what was in there before you went shopping. This helps you be more resourceful and less wasteful in the kitchen.

3. **Being less wasteful in the kitchen is also about being aware of your surroundings.** If you see something is getting a little too ripe, prep it to be frozen. For example, if you have strawberries or bananas that are almost past expiration, slice them up and freeze them for smoothies, homemade sorbet, or even fresh muffins on a Sunday morning. Celery, carrots, and onions freeze very well. If they're starting to get soft, you can peel and dice them, then transfer 1-cup portions into zip-top bags and freeze. Pull out a few bags to use for recipes throughout the month.

4. **Fresh herbs can be dried and stored in mason jars.** Don't let your herbs go to waste! Freezing is one way to preserve herbs, but they can also be dried using the microwave or the oven. This is my favorite trick when I have a small amount of herbs and want to dry them right away. Wash and dry them very well. (Excess moisture will steam them instead of dry them.) Remove the leaves of herbs like rosemary or thyme from stems. (A more tender herb like

parsley or cilantro can stay as is.) Lay the herbs in a single layer between two paper towels on a microwave-safe plate and microwave in 30 second intervals, checking after each round. Most herbs will fully dry in 2 minutes and you'll know they're ready when their leaves become brittle and crumble easily between your fingers. Let them cool, then crumble them, and then store in an airtight jar.

5. **Save old jars.** This is something my Nonna taught me. You don't have to save every jar, just the useful ones. Many of the condiments you buy on the regular come in great jars. I will save these jars and repurpose them for food storage. There's really nothing like a nice jar with a tight-fitting lid. Plastic containers are known to be toxic in some cases, and who wants to microwave their food in plastic anyway? Why not repurpose jars that you're paying for already when you're buying these condiments from the grocery store? Sometimes you just need to think outside of the box.

6. **Try to build meals out of your leftovers.** What do I have in my fridge and what could I make with it? For example, if you have a bunch of leftover vegetables, why not make them into a frittata? Leftover mashed potatoes? You could make shepherd's pie or even homemade gnocchi. Leftover cured meats and cheeses from last night's charcuterie board? Make antipasto salad. Again, stay creative in the kitchen and your waste will diminish.

Mains

SERVES	PREP	COOK	TOTAL
4	10 minutes	50 minutes	1 hour

Bone-in Pork Chops with Vinegar Peppers

Growing up in my Italian American household, my mother would vinegar pepper ANYTHING! I mean, I am not mad at it because these delicious peppers are usually pickled and packed in vinegar, which helps tenderize the pork chops nicely. Our favorite variation was always a nice thick-cut bone-in pork chop but it is also great with chicken thighs! The recipe is similar—just swap out the pork chops for bone-in chicken thighs and adjust the cooking time as needed.

4 thick bone-in pork chops (about 1.5-inch or 4 cm thick)

Salt and freshly ground pepper, to taste

3 tablespoons extra-virgin olive oil, divided

1 large yellow onion, thinly sliced (about 2 cups)

1 small red bell pepper, thinly sliced (about ¾ cup)

1x 32-ounce (907 g) jar of whole hot or sweet cherry peppers, such as Cento Hot

6 garlic cloves, thinly sliced

Chopped parsley, for garnish

1. Season both sides of the bone-in pork chops with salt and pepper.

2. Heat 1 tablespoon olive oil in a large skillet set over medium-high heat. You will know the oil is hot once you see ripples in the pan. Add the seasoned pork chops. We are not cooking the pork chops here; we just want to get a nice sear on them. This will build flavor! Cook for 4 minutes. Flip and cook for an additional 4 minutes. Remove the pork chops from the pan and set aside.

3. Reduce the heat to medium-low and add the remaining 2 tablespoons oil.

4. Add the onions and bell peppers. Cook for about 10 minutes until caramelized. Add the cherry peppers in liquid and garlic. Stir. Simmer on low for 3 to 5 minutes.

5. Add the pork chops back in and nestle them in the vegetables. Cover with a tight-fitting lid. Cook on the stovetop for about 25 minutes.

6. Rest for 5 minutes before serving,

7. Garnish with chopped parsley and enjoy!

Notes

- I love to serve this with my Semi-Semolina Loaf (see page 150 and a simple arugula salad dressed with fresh lemon juice and extra-virgin olive oil. The fresh bread will soak up those delicious juices and the pepperiness from the arugula really complements the whole dish.
- If you are using chicken thighs, adjust Step 5 and cook for 50 minutes rather than 25 minutes.

SERVES	PREP	COOK	TOTAL
4 to 6	15 minutes	1 hour 15 minutes	1 hour 30 minutes

Savory Braised Chicken Thighs

This recipe is an easy, one-pan dish that works well with any cut of chicken. I prefer (and recommend) bone-in, skin-on chicken thighs. They're humble, forgiving, and friggin' delicious when you give them the love they deserve. This is the kind of dish that brings me back to my grandma's kitchen. The smell alone makes you want to set the table with fine China. Serve this over a bowl of capellini—and don't forget the crusty semolina to sop up that savory tomato sauce.

8 bone-in, skin-on chicken thighs, about 5-6 ounces (140-170 g) each

Salt and freshly ground black pepper

3 tablespoons extra-virgin olive oil, divided

1x 2-ounce (57 g) can of anchovies, thoroughly drained

1 small white onion, sliced (about ½ cup)

1 yellow bell pepper, sliced (about ½ cup)

1 fennel bulb, sliced (about ½ cup)

½ cup red wine

5 garlic cloves, thinly sliced

½ cup sun-dried tomatoes, thinly sliced

1x 28-ounce (793 g) can crushed tomatoes

1 tablespoon raw honey

⅓ cup pitted Castelvetrano olives

3 tablespoons capers

4 basil leaves

Juice of ½ lemon

Chopped parsley, for garnish

1. Liberally season the chicken thighs with salt and pepper.

2. Heat 2 tablespoons olive oil in a large, oven-safe skillet over medium heat. Add the chicken thighs, skin-side down, and cook for 8 to 10 minutes per side. Remove from the pan and set aside.

3. Reduce the heat to low and add in the remaining olive oil and the anchovies. Cook for 3 to 5 minutes.

4. Add the onions, peppers, and fennel. Cook for 10 to 12 minutes until caramelized.

5. Add the red wine, garlic, sun-dried tomatoes, crushed tomatoes, and honey. Stir.

6. Nestle the chicken thighs in the sauce, skin-side up.

7. Add in the olives and capers. Sprinkle the basil on top, cover, and simmer for 40 minutes.

8. Remove the saucepan from the stovetop and remove the cover. Broil in the oven for 3 to 5 minutes until the chicken skin is caramelized.

9. To finish, squeeze fresh lemon juice on top and garnish with chopped parsley.

SERVES	PREP	COOK	TOTAL
4 to 6	15 minutes	1 hour 10 minutes	1 hour 25 minutes

Mommy's Special Roasted Chicken Legs

My girls love this meal so much that they request it at least once a week. To tell you the truth, it's just a sheet pan dinner I created to utilize the "First In, First Out (FIFO)" method of using up what you already have before moving on to newer items. Most people have some cut of chicken on hand; with a little help from your condiment stash, you can create a flavorful dish. During the week, there's nothing I love more than a one-pan meal. Chicken legs are so underrated—they are flavorful, versatile, and affordable! I promise that you and your kiddos will love this one. This dish really is proof that simple ingredients can create unforgettable meals.

8 bone-in, skin-on chicken legs

1 large carrot, diced

1 medium white onion, sliced

1 orange bell pepper, deseeded and sliced

3 yellow potatoes, cut into wedges

2 bulbs of garlic

½ cup Italian dressing

2 tablespoons extra-virgin olive oil

2 tablespoons balsamic vinegar

2 thyme sprigs

Salt and freshly ground black pepper, to taste

½ cup white wine

Chopped parsley, for garnish (optional)

1. Preheat the oven to 400°F (200°C).
2. Arrange the chicken legs, carrots, onions, bell peppers, and potatoes in a single layer on a large baking sheet.
3. Slice about ½ inch (13 mm) off the top of the garlic heads. Place the garlic on the baking sheet, cut-side up.
4. In a medium mixing bowl, whisk together the Italian dressing, olive oil, balsamic vinegar, thyme (stems removed), salt, and pepper. Pour over the chicken and vegetables and toss to combine.
5. Cover with foil and bake for 45 minutes.
6. Remove the foil and increase the heat to 425°F (220°C).
7. Deglaze the baking sheet with white wine and bake for 25 minutes, uncovered.
8. Remove from the oven and let rest. Squeeze out the roasted garlic cloves and serve with the roasted vegetables on the pan.
9. Garnish with chopped parsley, if desired.

Notes

- You can use chicken stock in place of the white wine.
- I like to serve this chicken with arugula dressed with freshly squeezed lemon juice and olive oil.

SERVES	PREP	COOK	TOTAL
4	10 minutes	1 hour 15 minutes	1 hour 25 minutes

Sausage, Peppers, and Onions

This meal will forever remind me of a summer night, walking the neighborhood Italian feast. We used to get all dolled up to eat sausage and pepper heroes. (Yes, it's a hero!) Of course everyone's mother makes it the best, but I am here to show you how to make it like your mother. I know the controversy is with sauce or without—we are definitely a "without sauce" household. This can be served on our Semi-Semolina Loaf (see page 158) over polenta, rice, or just as is!

4 garlic cloves, thinly sliced

3 yellow onions, thinly sliced (about 3 cups)

4 bell peppers, thinly sliced (about 4 cups)

6 tablespoons extra-virgin olive oil, divided

1 tablespoon red wine vinegar

Salt and freshly ground black pepper, to taste

8 Italian sausages, sweet or hot

Chopped parsley, for garnish

Lemon wedges, for garnish

Special Equipment

Deep 9 x 13-inch (23 x 33 cm) baking dish

1. Preheat the oven to 400°F (200°C).
2. In a deep 9 x 13-inch (23 x 33 cm) baking dish, add the garlic, onions, peppers, 4 tablespoons olive oil, the red wine vinegar, salt, and pepper. Toss to combine.
3. In a separate 9 x 13-inch (23 x 33 cm) baking dish, add the sausages and remaining 2 tablespoons olive oil.
4. Bake the vegetables and sausage for 1 hour, tossing every 15 minutes to ensure even cooking.
5. Transfer the sausage to a cutting board and let rest for 5 minutes.
6. Pour the accumulated cooking liquid from the sausage on top of the roasted onions and peppers.
7. Slice the sausages on a bias and transfer to the baking dish with the roasted vegetables. Mix well.
8. Bake for 15 minutes. Garnish with chopped parsley and freshly squeezed lemon juice.

SERVES	PREP	COOK	TOTAL
4 to 6	25 minutes	3 hours 35 minutes	4 hours

Garlic-Stuffed Roast Beef with Gravy

This garlic-stuffed roast beef is pure comfort! The hardest part of this recipe is waiting to slice and serve it. We are using an eye round, which is an affordable, lean cut of beef. To make it delicious, you'll need to season it liberally, avoid overcooking, and allow plenty of time for it to rest. This recipe is foolproof, and it comes out perfect every time!

3 pounds (1,360 g) eye of round roast

8 garlic cloves, thinly sliced

2 tablespoons extra-virgin olive oil, divided

Salt and freshly ground black pepper, to taste

¼ cup diced carrots

¼ cup diced celery

¼ cup diced yellow onion

¼ cup diced fennel

1½ cups beef stock, divided

2 tablespoons salted butter

2 tablespoons all-purpose flour

1 teaspoon Worcestershire sauce

Chopped parsley, for garnish (optional)

Special Equipment

Meat thermometer

Food processor

Roasting pan

1. Preheat the oven to 475°F (245°C).

2. Pat the roast dry with paper towels. Using a small sharp knife, make 1-inch (2.5 cm) deep slits into the roast all over. Insert the sliced garlic into each slit. Make sure you fully push the garlic in the slit to ensure it doesn't burn.

3. Rub the roast with 1 tablespoon olive oil. Season liberally with salt and pepper, making sure all sides are coated. Set aside.

4. Add the carrots, celery, onion, and fennel to a large, shallow roasting pan. Pour the remaining olive oil and ½ cup beef stock over the vegetables. Season with salt and pepper and arrange them in the center of the roasting pan. Place the roast on top of the bed of vegetables. Bake for about 27 minutes. Turn the oven off and do not open the door for 3 hours, until the internal temperature reaches 135°F (57°C).

5. Transfer the vegetables and drippings to the bowl of a food processor fitted with the blade attachment. Process until smooth and set aside.

6. Melt the butter in a medium saucepan over medium-low heat. Add the flour and whisk to combine. Cook for 2 to 3 minutes, whisking often, until light brown.

7. Slowly add in the remaining beef stock and whisk until smooth and creamy.

8. Add the puréed vegetables and Worcestershire sauce. Cook for about 5 minutes, whisking often, until the gravy thickens.

9. I love to finish this gravy by stirring in some freshly chopped parsley for a pop of color and freshness, but that is totally optional! Slice the roast against the grain and serve with my Butter Poached Garlic Mashed Potatoes (see page 107) and a bright green salad.

Notes

- Cook the roast for 8 minutes per pound for rare or 9 minutes per pound for medium-rare.
- Whatever size roast you're cooking, be sure to let it rest in the oven for 3 hours.

SERVES	PREP	COOK	TOTAL
4 or 5	20 minutes	40 minutes	1 hour

Prosciutto and Fontina Chicken Rollatini

This is one of those recipes that you need under your belt. The flavor combination possibilities are endless here. The base for this recipe is thinly sliced chicken breast, which is stuffed, breaded, and fried until golden brown. The savory pan sauce helps to keep everything moist. The salty prosciutto pairs perfectly with the buttery fontina. It's easy enough for a weeknight but also delicious enough for a holiday dinner.

3 boneless, skinless chicken breasts, about 5 ounces (140 g) each

½ cup grated Pecorino Romano

½ cup seasoned breadcrumbs

1 teaspoon garlic powder

1 teaspoon onion powder

2 tablespoons chopped parsley, plus more for garnish

Salt and freshly ground black pepper

5 tablespoons extra-virgin olive oil, divided

9 slices prosciutto

9 slices Fontina

1 tablespoon salted butter

1 medium yellow onion, sliced (about 1 cup)

1 cup white wine

1 cup chicken stock

4 garlic cloves, minced

Special Equipment

Zip-top bag

Meat mallet

1. Cut the chicken breasts against the grain, lengthwise, into 3 equal pieces. Place the chicken in a large zip-top bag. Use a meat mallet to pound each piece until thin. Repeat with the other two breasts.

2. Remove the chicken from the bag and pat dry with paper towels. Set aside.

3. In a shallow bowl, add the Pecorino Romano, breadcrumbs, garlic powder, onion powder, parsley, salt, and pepper.

4. In another shallow bowl, add 4 tablespoons of the olive oil. Dip one cutlet in the olive oil, then into the breadcrumb mixture and coat evenly on both sides. Transfer to a baking sheet and repeat with the remaining chicken.

5. Place one slice of prosciutto on each cutlet, followed by a slice of Fontina. Roll tightly and place the cutlet seam side-down on the baking sheet.

6. Heat the remaining 1 tablespoon of olive oil in a large skillet set over medium heat. Working in batches, add the rollatini, seam side-down, and cook for about 2 minutes per side until golden brown and crispy. Set aside.

7. In the same skillet, melt the butter. Add the onions and cook for 10 to 12 minutes, stirring often, until caramelized. Add the white wine, chicken stock, and garlic. Place the rollatini in the skillet, seam side-down. Reduce the heat to medium-low and cook for about 20 minutes until the chicken is cooked through and the sauce has thickened.

8. Garnish with fresh chopped parsley. Serve with a side of Brown Butter Polenta (see page 103).

SERVES	PREP	COOK	TOTAL
4	10 minutes (plus at least 8 hours to marinate, best overnight)	8 minutes	8½ hours

Hoisin-Marinated Flap Steak

Flap steak, which is also known as sirloin tip or bavette, is so rich and flavorful. It's like skirt steak but half the price! It's a cut of beef that loves to be marinated and cooked at a high temperature. This makes it perfect for grilling season or even a quick sear under the broiler during those colder months. A hoisin marinade is perfect for this tender cut of beef. I love to serve this with sticky white rice and marinated cucumbers.

1½ pounds (681 g) flap steak

3 garlic cloves, minced

2 scallions, sliced

1 teaspoon fresh ginger, minced

1 tablespoon sesame oil

1 tablespoon rice wine vinegar

½ cup hoisin sauce

¼ cup seasoned soy sauce

Juice of 1 mandarin orange

Special Equipment

Zip-top bag

Grill

Meat thermometer

1. Place the flap steak in a large zip-top bag.

2. In a large bowl, whisk together the garlic, scallions, ginger, sesame oil, rice wine vinegar, hoisin sauce, seasoned soy sauce, and mandarin orange juice.

3. Pour over your steak, chill, and marinate for at least 8 hours, preferably overnight.

4. Bring the steak to room temperature before cooking, about 30 minutes.

5. Heat the grill to high. Grill the steak for 3 to 4 minutes per side or until the internal temperature reaches 125°F to 130°F (51°C to 54°C).

6. Let the steak rest for 8 minutes. Slice against the grain.

Notes

- I usually find seasoned soy sauce at my local Asian market. If you can't find it, you can use regular soy sauce plus 1 tablespoon of honey or brown sugar.
- You can use a few tablespoons of fresh orange, lemon, or lime juice in place of the mandarin orange juice.
- To cook under the broiler: Preheat the broiler to high and roast the steak for 6 minutes. Flip and roast for another 6 minutes. Let it rest for 8 minutes before slicing and serving.

SERVES	PREP	COOK	TOTAL
4	15 minutes	10 minutes	25 minutes

Seared Salmon with Plum Salsa

I hear a lot of people saying they aren't huge fans of salmon. I think they just aren't cooking it properly. I love frying it up in a hot pan with some butter, garlic, fresh herbs—and to baste it like a steak. The key is to cook it about 80% on one side to create a crispy texture. That paired with a bright and citrusy plum salsa is a match made in heaven. Fruit salsas are also a great way to use what produce you have on hand and to incorporate a fresh element to your meals. I like to serve this with a lightly dressed arugula salad.

3 ripe plums, diced

1 plum tomato, diced

¼ red onion, diced

2 jalapeño peppers, ribs and seeds removed, diced

1 mini cucumber, diced

1 avocado, diced

¼ cup chopped cilantro

Juice of 2 limes

1 teaspoon honey

3 tablespoons extra-virgin olive oil, divided

Salt and freshly ground pepper, to taste

4x 6-ounce (170 g) skin-on salmon fillets

2 tablespoon salted butter

3 garlic cloves

1 rosemary sprig

1 parsley sprig

Special Equipment

Cast-iron skillet

1. In a large bowl, combine the plums, plum tomato, red onion, jalapeños, cucumber, avocado, cilantro, lime juice, honey, and 1 tablespoon olive oil. Season to taste with salt and pepper. Set aside.

2. Pat the salmon dry with paper towels. Season both sides evenly with salt and pepper.

3. In a large cast-iron skillet set over high heat, add the remaining 2 tablespoons olive oil and the butter.

4. Once the pan starts to smoke and the butter is just turning brown, add the salmon flesh-side down, garlic, rosemary, and parsley. Cook for 4 to 5 minutes.

5. Flip the salmon. Use a spoon to gently pour the garlic herb butter over the salmon and baste for 2 to 3 minutes. Transfer the salmon to a plate, cover lightly with foil, and let rest for 5 minutes.

6. Top with plum salsa and serve flesh-side up. Enjoy!

MAKES	PREP	COOK	TOTAL
18 meatballs	45 minutes	1 hour	1 hour 45 minutes

Classic Meatballs with Marinara Sauce

I truly feel that everyone walking this earth should know how to make a delicious meatball. It is so versatile and can be served so many ways—not just on top of spaghetti. Making meatballs should be easy and therapeutic! These are baked in the oven first and finished off in a chunky marinara sauce. They are perfect for any weeknight meal or Sunday dinner.

For the meatballs

1 cup firmly packed stale bread cubes (about 2 pieces; any bread will work)

¼ cup whole milk

1 pound (454 g) ground beef

¾ cup grated Pecorino Romano

2 large eggs

2 tablespoons chopped parsley

2 tablespoons chopped basil

Salt and freshly ground pepper, to taste

For the marinara sauce

2 tablespoons extra-virgin olive oil, divided

1 small yellow onion, finely diced (about ¾ cup)

8 garlic cloves, minced

1x 28-ounce (793 g) can diced tomatoes

1x 28-ounce (793 g) can crushed tomatoes

4 basil leaves

Salt and freshly ground pepper, to taste

Special Equipment

Parchment paper

Large cookie scoop (#20)

1. Preheat the oven to 375°F (190°C).

2. In a large bowl, combine the bread and milk, set aside.

3. Make the marinara sauce: Heat the olive oil in a large skillet set over medium heat. Add the onions and garlic and cook for about 8 minutes. Remove half of the onion and garlic mixture and set aside.

4. Add the diced tomatoes, crushed tomatoes, basil leaves, salt, and pepper to the skillet. Stir. Bring the sauce up to a simmer, then reduce the heat to low, cover, and cook.

5. Meanwhile, make the meatballs: In a large bowl, add the ground beef, stale bread and milk mixture, reserved onions and garlic, Pecorino Romano, eggs, parsley, basil, salt, and pepper. Mix until just combined.

6. Line a large baking sheet with parchment paper and drizzle with the olive oil.

7. Use a large cookie scoop (#20 scoop; 3 tablespoons) to form the meatballs. Roll around in your palm for a few seconds and place evenly on your baking sheet.

8. Bake for 20 minutes, turning halfway through.

9. Remove the lid from your simmering sauce and gently add the meatballs. Cover and cook for 30 minutes. This is the type of sauce that really only needs an hour and a half, but you can simmer it longer and the flavor will only get better!

Notes

- I like to serve these meatballs over spaghetti or even with a nice Semi-Semolina Loaf (see page 158).
- I love to make a huge batch of these meatballs and freeze half before adding to the sauce. Take the desired number of meatballs you want to freeze and place in a single layer on a baking sheet. Freeze until solid and then add the frozen meatballs to a zip-top bag. These will last in your freezer for up to 6 months. Your future self will thank you when that busy weeknight hits and you have fresh meatballs in your freezer!

MAKES	PREP	COOK	TOTAL
About 30 meatballs	20 minutes	1 hour 15 minutes	1 hour 35 minutes

French Onion Chicken Meatballs with Mushroom Gravy

This is one of those seriously delicious semi-homemade recipes (shout-out to you, Sandra Lee!). This recipe starts with slowly caramelized onions—and I am going to teach you a little trick to speed up that process. This recipe is my playful twist on two childhood classics—fried meatballs and French onion soup! The homemade mushroom gravy ties it all together and every bite really tastes like pure comfort.

6 tablespoons salted butter, divided

3 large yellow onions, thinly sliced (about 5 cups)

1 pound (454 g) ground chicken

4 garlic cloves, minced

¼ cup grated Pecorino Romano

½ cup shredded Gruyère

¼ cup seasoned panko breadcrumbs

1 tablespoon chopped parsley, plus more for garnish

2 large eggs

Salt and freshly ground pepper, to taste

1 tablespoon extra-virgin olive oil

20 ounces (567 g) sliced mushrooms, such as baby bella or button

3 tablespoons all-purpose flour

¼ cup chicken stock

2 cups whole milk

1 tablespoon chopped parsley

Special Equipment

Small cookie scoop (#40)

1. Heat 3 tablespoons butter in a large skillet set over medium heat. Add the onions and 3 tablespoons water. Cover and cook for 30 minutes, stirring occasionally. Set aside to cool completely.

2. In a large bowl, add the chicken, garlic, Pecorino Romano, Gruyère, breadcrumbs, parsley, eggs, salt, and pepper to taste. Mix to combine. Add the caramelized onions and mix until just combined.

3. Preheat the oven to 425°F (220°C).

4. Drizzle the olive oil evenly over a large baking sheet. Use a small cookie scoop (#40; 2 tablespoons) to form the meatballs and place on the prepared baking sheet.

5. Bake for 15 to 18 minutes. In the same skillet you cooked the caramelized onions, add the remaining 3 tablespoons butter and thinly sliced mushrooms. Season to taste with salt and pepper. Cook for about 15 minutes until they have reduced by about half.

6. Sprinkle the flour over the mushrooms. Cook for 2 minutes, stirring constantly.

7. Slowly add the chicken stock and whole milk, whisking constantly. Season to taste with salt and pepper.

8. Add the cooked meatballs to the gravy. Cook for about 12 minutes, basting the gravy over the meatballs. Garnish with chopped parsley.

Note

- Serve the meatballs over Butter Poached Garlic Mashed Potatoes (see page 107) or good ol' buttered egg noodles with a bright green salad on the side.

SERVES	PREP	COOK	TOTAL
6	30 minutes	1 hour 30 minutes	2 hours

Meatball and Vegetable Stew

You've probably had beef stew before, but have you ever had meatball stew? This nostalgic, comforting dish can be made with fresh or frozen meatballs. I prefer to cook this stew in a Dutch oven, but it can easily be made in a slow cooker, which makes it a great weeknight meal. This is my favorite vegetable combination but don't be afraid to improvise if you have other produce on hand.

20 Classic Meatballs (see page 43)

3 tablespoon plus 1 teaspoon extra-virgin olive oil, divided

1x 20-ounce (567 g) carton baby bella mushrooms, halved

2 carrots, sliced (about 1 cup)

2 celery stalks, sliced (about 1 cup)

1 fennel bulb, sliced (about 1 cup)

4 garlic cloves, smashed

1x 28-ounce (793 g) can crushed tomatoes

3½ cups beef stock

1 tablespoon soy sauce

12 yellow baby potatoes, halved (about 2 cups)

1 rosemary sprig

1 thyme sprig

Pecorino Romano rind (about 2 inches; 5 cm)

2 tablespoons chopped parsley

2 cups arugula

Juice of ½ lemon (about 2 tablespoons)

Salt and freshly ground pepper, to taste

1. Prepare the Classic Meatballs (see page 43).

2. Heat 1 tablespoon oil in a large, deep pot set over medium heat. Add the mushrooms and cook for about 10 minutes until golden brown. Remove from the pot and set aside.

3. Add remaining oil to the pot and heat. Add the carrots, celery, fennel, and garlic and cook for about 14 minutes until golden brown.

4. Add the crushed tomatoes, beef stock, and soy sauce. Simmer for 3 to 4 minutes.

5. Add the meatballs, potatoes, rosemary, thyme, and Pecorino Romano rind. Bring the mixture to a simmer, then reduce the heat to low, cover, and cook for about 1 hour.

6. Remove from the heat and stir in the parsley and mushrooms.

7. In a medium bowl, add the arugula, lemon juice, and 1 teaspoon olive oil and toss to combine. Season to taste with salt and pepper.

8. Serve the stew in a bowl as is, on a bed of rice, or with my kids' favorite—ditalini. Top with a handful of the dressed arugula and enjoy my childhood in a bowl!

Notes

- You can make this exact meal with 1 pound of chuck roast. Instead of preparing the meatballs, sear the cubed chuck roast instead! Remove from the pan and set aside for later. Add the meat back in when the recipe directs you to add in your meatballs and cook for 3 hours, rather than 1 hour.
- To make this recipe in a slow cooker, sear the vegetables first and add to the slow cooker. Follow the rest of the recipe instructions. Cook on low for 4 hours.
- Pecorino Romano or Parmigiano-Reggiano rinds can be found in the cheese section of most grocery stores. You can store those in your freezer and add to stews, soups, and sauces. It's also not the end of the world if you can't find them! You can add two anchovies instead, which will produce that same nutty, umami flavor that the rind will give you. And NO, it won't taste like anchovies.

SERVES	PREP	COOK	TOTAL
6	15 minutes (plus 40 minutes to roast garlic)	1 hour 15 minutes	2 hours 10 minutes

Braised and Stuffed Cubanelle Peppers

The combination of roasted garlic and Italian sausage steals the show here. This is one of those recipes that I make an abundance of. To make ahead, I recommend wrapping and freezing the peppers raw before you put them in the marinara. It's great for meal prep or if you just want to treat yourself to something different than what everybody else wants for dinner. You can swap out the type of meat here; it works great with ground chicken or ground beef. You could even swap out the type of pepper—I love using a long hot or a sweet banana pepper.

1 head of garlic

1 tablespoon extra-virgin olive oil

3 tablespoons salted butter

½ cup diced white onion

8 baby bella mushrooms, chopped

1 cup chopped baby spinach

1 pound (454 g) sweet (or hot) Italian sausage, casings removed

½ cup cooked white rice

1 tablespoon breadcrumbs

½ cup grated Pecorino Romano

½ cup diced mozzarella

1 large egg

2 tablespoons chopped parsley

Salt and freshly ground pepper, to taste

8 Cubanelle peppers, tops, ribs, and seeds removed

3 cups Homemade Marinara Sauce (see page 43)

1. Preheat the oven to 400°F (200°C).

2. Slice the top off the head of garlic to expose the cloves and place on top of a sheet of aluminum foil. Pour the olive oil all over the garlic. Wrap it tightly and place on a baking sheet. Bake for 40 minutes.

3. **Meanwhile, make the filling:** Line a plate with paper towel. Heat the butter in a large skillet over medium heat. Add the onions and mushrooms. Cook for about 15 minutes until reduced by half and caramelized.

4. Add the chopped spinach. Cook for about 1 minute, until wilted. Transfer the mixture to the prepared plate and cool.

5. In a large bowl, add the sausage. Squeeze all of the roasted garlic cloves into the bowl. Add the cooled vegetables, rice, breadcrumbs, Pecorino Romano, mozzarella, egg, and parsley. Season to taste with salt and pepper. Mix until well combined.

6. Reduce the oven to 350°F (180°C).

7. Stuff each pepper with the filling, pushing down as you go. Be gentle here because we want to try to keep the peppers whole.

8. In a large, oven-safe pot, add the marinara sauce. Nestle the stuffed peppers in the sauce in an upright position and cover.

9. Bake for 1 hour.

10. Remove from the oven and let rest for at least 10 minutes.

Note

- Serve with a piece of Semi-Semolina Loaf (see page 158) or over pasta.

MAKES	PREP	COOK	TOTAL
16 large arancini	1 hour	3 hours 25 minutes (plus cooling time for the pork)	4 hours 25 minutes

Pulled Pork Arancini

When I was a caterer, I used to make both sweet and savory rice balls (aka arancini). This version was our top seller—aside from our traditional meat-and-peas one. The rice is mixed with fried onions and a rich Irish cheddar, then is loaded with pulled pork! This is a great way to use up leftover rice or even leftover pulled pork. It's the perfect appetizer for game day or anytime you're trying to impress someone.

For the filling

1 pound (454 g) boneless country pork spareribs

1 small yellow onion, thinly sliced (about ½ cup)

4 garlic cloves, minced

Juice of 1 orange

½ cup barbecue sauce

½ cup Dr Pepper soda

Salt and freshly ground black pepper

For the rice mixture

2 tablespoons salted butter

1 medium yellow onion, thinly sliced (about 1 cup)

7 cups cooked short-grain rice (about 3 cups uncooked)

1 cup shredded cheddar (see Notes)

1 cup grated Pecorino Romano

¼ cup chopped parsley

2 large eggs

1 tablespoon garlic powder

1 tablespoon onion powder

Salt, to taste

1 teaspoon freshly ground pepper

2 cups seasoned panko breadcrumbs, preferably 4C brand

Light neutral oil for frying, such as avocado oil (about 4-6 cups)

Special Equipment

Dutch oven

Candy thermometer

Wire rack

1. Prepare the filling: Preheat the oven to 350°F (180°C). In a large baking dish, add the ribs, onions, garlic, orange juice, barbecue sauce, Dr Pepper, salt, and pepper.

2. Cover tightly with foil and roast for 3 hours until the meat is shreddable. Set aside to cool.

3. Make the rice mixture: Melt the butter in a medium pot set over medium heat. Add the onion and cook for about 15 minutes until softened and reduced in size. Set aside to cool.

4. In a large bowl, add the cooked rice, onions, shredded cheddar, Pecorino Romano, parsley, eggs, garlic powder, onion powder, salt, and pepper. Mix well.

5. In a separate medium bowl, add the breadcrumbs.

6. Heat about 4 inches (10 cm) of oil in a deep pot such as a Dutch oven until it reaches 375°F (190°C).

7. Take about 3 tablespoons of rice mixture into the palm of your hand and flatten into a disc.

8. Scoop 1 hefty tablespoon of the pulled pork mixture into the center of the rice in your palm. Mold the rice over the filling and roll into a ball.

9. Roll one arancini into the breadcrumbs and coat evenly on all sides. Set aside and repeat with the remaining arancini.

10. Working in batches, fry the arancini for 8 to 10 minutes each ball, turning occasionally to ensure even browning.

11. Transfer to a wire rack and immediately season with salt.

Notes

- Recommended brand for the cheddar: Kerrygold Dubliner
- These freeze GREAT! Wrap individually and freeze for up to 4 months.
- After roasting, if the pork ribs seem too dry, you can add more barbecue sauce until you reach your desired consistency.
- Serve these as the main event with a fresh green salad on the side or make them smaller for a bite-size appetizer.

Appetizers

SERVES	PREP	COOK	TOTAL
6	45 minutes (plus 12 hours to marinate)	25 minutes	13 hours 10 minutes

The Ultimate Seafood Salad

This isn't just a recipe, it's a tradition. So many families I know make their own version of seafood salad (insalata di mare) for Christmas Eve, and no two are alike. My grandmother prepared hers one way, my mom prepared hers another way, and now this one is all mine. The secret? Cooking each type of seafood separately so nothing overcooks and letting it all sit overnight so the flavors marry.

For the poaching liquid

4 cups water

½ cup clam juice

½ cup dry white wine

½ cup fresh orange juice

½ yellow onion, halved

1 fennel top, halved

3 garlic cloves, smashed

2 sprigs rosemary

2 sprigs thyme

1 tablespoon salt

For the seafood salad

¾ pound (340 g) shrimp, cleaned

½ pound (227 g) calamari, cleaned and cut into rings/tentacles

½ pound (227 g) baby octopus

½ pound (227 g) bay scallops

2 small lobster tails (about 1 pound; 454 g), shelled and cut into bite-size pieces

½ pound (227 g) mussel meat (1 pound/454 g shelled)

2 garlic cloves, finely minced

½ small red onion, thinly sliced

½ bulb fennel, thinly sliced

2 celery stalks, thinly sliced

½ red bell pepper, ribs and seeds removed, finely chopped

½ Meyer lemon, quartered then thinly sliced

¼ cup Castelvetrano olives, halved

½ cup chopped parsley

½ cup torn basil

½ cup lemon juice (from about 3 lemons)

½ cup extra-virgin olive oil, plus more to taste

2 tablespoons white wine vinegar

½ teaspoon dried oregano

Salt and freshly ground black pepper, to taste

Arugula, for serving (optional)

1. Prepare the poaching liquid: In a large pot over medium heat, combine the water, clam juice, white wine, orange juice, onion, fennel, garlic, rosemary, thyme, and salt and bring to a gentle simmer, not a boil.

2. Set up a fine-mesh sieve, small colander, or steaming basket to lower seafood in and out easily. We will be poaching each seafood in batches. (The following poaching instructions are for smaller cuts and pieces of seafood. Make sure not to overcrowd the pot.)

3. Prepare the seafood salad: Lower the shrimp into the simmering liquid. Poach for 3 minutes until just pink and slightly firm. Remove and add to a large bowl.

4. Lower in the calamari for about 2 minutes until opaque. Remove and add to the bowl.

5. Lower in the baby octopus and poach 6 minutes, or until fork-tender. Remove and add to the bowl.

6. Lower in the bay scallops and poach for 2 minutes. Remove and add to the bowl.

7. Lower in the lobster tails and poach for 3 minutes until opaque and firm. Remove and add to the bowl.

8. Lower in the cooked mussels and poach for 2 minutes. Remove and add to the bowl.

9. In a separate large bowl, combine the garlic, red onion, fennel, celery, red bell pepper, lemon, olives, parsley, basil, lemon juice, olive oil, white wine vinegar, oregano, salt, and pepper, then mix in with the poached seafood in the first bowl.

10. Gently toss to coat. Make sure you're tasting as you go and adjusting seasonings as needed.

11. Chill in the fridge for at least 12 hours and then toss again before serving. Taste once more and adjust as needed before serving cold over some fresh arugula.

SERVES	PREP	COOK	TOTAL
8	10 minutes (plus 4 hours to marinate)	1 hour 5 minutes	5 hours 15 minutes

Sweet and Sour Roasted Peppers

This sweet and savory condiment is very popular in my house—especially in the summer with those gorgeous garden peppers. I normally use red bell peppers here, but any color can work. This Sicilian-style pepper dish works great as an appetizer but can also be used to flavor stews, to top pizza, or even as a base for a froscia! I love to make a big batch of these because of how useful they can be.

3 red bell peppers, ribs and seeds removed, cut into 1-inch (2.5 cm) strips (about 4 cups)

½ cup extra-virgin olive oil

5 garlic cloves, peeled and smashed

Salt and freshly ground black pepper, to taste

1 tablespoon red wine vinegar

¼ cup pine nuts

2 tablespoons raisins

1 tablespoon chopped parsley

Special Equipment

8 x 8-inch (20 x 20 cm) baking dish

1. Preheat the oven to 400°F (200°C).
2. In an 8 x 8-inch (20 x 20 cm) baking dish, add the bell peppers, olive oil, garlic, salt, and pepper.
3. Cover and cook for 1 hour. Once they are done, reserve 1 tablespoon of oil and remove and discard the garlic.
4. Add the red wine vinegar to the peppers. Stir. Set aside.
5. Transfer the reserved oil to a small skillet. Add the pine nuts and toast for 3 to 5 minutes.
6. Transfer the toasted pine nuts to the pepper mixture. Add the raisins and parsley. Toss.

Notes

- I recommend making this at least 4 hours before you want to enjoy it. The longer it marinates the better it is.
- Take out of the fridge at least a half hour before you want to enjoy; stir to incorporate the oil.

Storage Tip

- Store in your fridge in a tightly sealed mason jar and this will stay delicious for at least 10 days.

MAKES	PREP	COOK	TOTAL
About 3 cups	10 minutes	1 hour	1 hour 10 minutes

Confit Cherry Tomato Relish

I grew up in a kitchen where nothing went to waste, especially during gardening season. Cherry tomatoes were always in abundance and my nonna was always creating new ways to use them. Lucky for us, she had me in the kitchen nine times out of ten putting me to work! So now here we are, recreating my nonna's recipes with my own little twist. This works great as a spread for crostini, as a filling in our Savory Thumbprint Cookies (see page 68), or even as the base to a chilled pasta salad!

1 cup extra-virgin olive oil

2x 10-ounce (283 g) containers cherry tomatoes

15 garlic cloves

1 red onion, rough chop (about ½ cup)

1 tablespoon balsamic vinegar

1 tablespoon honey

1 sprig rosemary

4 fresh basil leaves

1 sprig parsley

1 sprig oregano

Salt and freshly ground black pepper, to taste

Special Equipment

9 x 13-inch (23 x 33 cm) baking dish

1. Preheat the oven to 400°F (200°C).

2. In a 9 x 13-inch (23 x 33 cm) baking dish, add the olive oil, cherry tomatoes, garlic, red onion, balsamic vinegar, honey, rosemary, basil, parsley, and oregano. Season to taste with salt and pepper.

3. Cover with foil and bake for 30 minutes.

4. After 30 minutes, uncover and cook for 30 minutes more.

5. Let rest for 5 minutes before serving. Discard the stems, then serve immediately or transfer to a jar and refrigerate for up to one week.

SERVES	PREP	COOK	TOTAL
10	30 minutes	50 minutes	1 hour 20 minutes

Eggplant Caponata

Caponata is a Sicilian dish that perfectly balances sweet and sour flavors. It is a great addition to your antipasto plate and is even better served on top of some crusty bread. This flavorful vegetable stew can be enjoyed as an appetizer, condiment, or even as a stuffing for chicken or fish. This dish is usually served at room temperature, and the flavor only improves with time, making this a perfect make-ahead dish for any occasion.

Salt, to taste

3 small eggplants, diced into 1-inch pieces (about 4 cups)

¾ cup extra-virgin olive oil, divided

¼ cup pine nuts

1 red bell pepper, diced (about 1 cup)

1 red onion, diced (about 1 cup)

2 celery stalks, sliced (about 1 cup)

3 tomatoes on the vine, diced (about 2 cups)

¼ cup balsamic vinegar

1 tablespoon honey (or any sweetener of your choice)

2 tablespoons golden raisins

¼ cup pitted Castelvetrano olives, halved (about 8 olives)

1 tablespoon capers

Freshly ground black pepper, to taste

1 tablespoon chopped parsley

1 tablespoon chopped basil

1. Preheat the oven to 400°F (200°C). Line a baking sheet with paper towel.

2. Salt the eggplant and let it rest on the prepared baking sheet to sweat.

3. In a small frying pan, heat 1 tablespoon olive oil. Add the pine nuts and cook for 3 to 4 minutes, stirring frequently, until toasted. Set aside.

4. Transfer the eggplant to another baking sheet and discard the paper towel. Drizzle with 3 tablespoons olive oil and toss to combine.

5. Bake for 15 minutes, flipping halfway through.

6. Heat ½ cup olive oil in a large skillet set over medium heat.

7. Add the bell peppers, onions, and celery and cook for about 15 minutes.

8. Add the tomatoes and cook for about 10 minutes, stirring occasionally.

9. Deglaze the pan with balsamic vinegar and honey. Simmer for about 5 minutes.

10. Add the raisins, olives, capers, and toasted pine nuts. Remove from heat. Season to taste with salt and pepper.

11. Allow to cool completely before adding the parsley and basil. Serve with crusty bread like my Semi-Semolina Loaf (see page 158).

Note

- Take the caponata out of the fridge about 30 minutes before serving because the olive oil will naturally congeal.

Storage Tip

- This will last in the fridge for up to 7 days or in the freezer for up to 3 months.

SERVES	PREP	COOK	TOTAL
10	20 minutes	1 hour	1 hour 20 minutes (plus 1 hour cooling time)

Cheesy Zucchini Pie

This is a family-favorite recipe, and we serve it as an appetizer every year, at every holiday! It is a classic dish that is easy to make and even easier to enjoy. I love to make this when hosting because it can be made in advance and served at room temperature. In fact, I recommend that it be served that way. This is a great way to use up an abundance of zucchini during gardening season, but it really is great all year round.

Cooking spray, for greasing

4 medium-size zucchini, diced small (about 4 cups)

1 small white onion, diced small (about ½ cup)

½ cup (8 tablespoons) salted butter

4 large eggs

1 cup pancake mix

1 cup shredded mozzarella

½ cup grated Pecorino Romano

1 teaspoon garlic powder

1 teaspoon onion powder

¼ cup parsley

Salt and freshly ground pepper, to taste

Special Equipment

10 x 12-inch (25 x 30 cm) baking dish

1. Preheat the oven 350°F (180°C). Grease a 10 x 12-inch (25 x 30 cm) baking dish. Set aside.
2. Pat the diced zucchini and onion dry with a paper towel.
3. Melt the stick of butter and set aside.
4. In a large bowl, combine the zucchini, onions, eggs, pancake mix, mozzarella, Pecorino Romano, melted butter, garlic powder, onion powder, parsley, salt, and pepper.
5. Transfer the mixture to the prepared baking dish and smooth into an even layer.
6. Bake for 1 hour, rotating the pan halfway through to ensure even cooking.
7. Let cool for at least 1 hour before slicing.

Notes

- This can be made using any variety of zucchini.
- The cheese here is interchangeable. A lot of times I use whatever cheese I have in my fridge, but this combo here is the best.

SERVES
6

PREP
30 minutes (plus at least 3 hours to marinate)

TOTAL
3 hours 30 minutes

The Ultimate Antipasto Salad

I vividly remember walking up to the deli counter and seeing that meat and cheese salad behind the glass. I loved it, but my mom always told me to make my own because the one in the stores is usually made up of leftovers. Years later, I appreciate that advice and totally agree. I re-created it with high-quality ingredients and tons of flavor. It can be altered to accommodate your taste buds, but here is my favorite combination.

½ cup diced Genoa salami (1-inch (2.5 cm) dice)

½ cup diced pepperoni (1-inch (2.5 cm) dice)

½ cup diced prosciutto di Parma (1-inch (2.5 cm) dice)

½ cup diced provolone (1-inch (2.5 cm) dice)

½ cup fresh mozzarella pearls

¼ cup marinated mushrooms

¼ cup giardiniera

¼ cup sliced sun-dried tomatoes

¼ cup sliced sweet cherry peppers

1x 6-ounce (170 g) can black olives, drained

2 tablespoons diced red onion

2 garlic cloves, minced

3 tablespoons extra-virgin olive oil

3 tablespoons white wine vinegar

2 tablespoons chopped parsley

2 tablespoons chopped basil

1 cup fresh arugula, for serving (optional)

1. In a large bowl, combine the salami, pepperoni, prosciutto di Parma, provolone, mozzarella pearls, mushrooms, giardiniera, sun-dried tomatoes, cherry peppers, olives, red onion, garlic, olive oil, white wine vinegar, parsley, and basil.

2. Cover and store in the fridge for at least 3 hours to marinate before serving.

3. Serve over a bed of plain arugula, if desired.

Note

- I love making this on a holiday and skipping the charcuterie board!

Storage Tip

- You can make this in advance and keep it in the fridge for up to 7 days.

SERVES	PREP	COOK	TOTAL
8	15 minutes	1 hour	1 hour 15 minutes

The Ultimate Shrimp Quiche

Nothing says Christmas morning like a shrimp quiche! My mother used to make this using the leftover shrimp from Christmas Eve. This is also a great recipe to save you from that last-minute brunch that you have planned. The egg mixture for this cheesy quiche is made in the blender so it makes for a beautiful texture. Shrimp paired with fried onions and peppers baked into a buttery crust—how can you go wrong? We are using a store-bought pie crust sheet here and I know you have one deep down in your freezer that's screaming to be used. I like to serve it with a light arugula salad for brunch.

1 tablespoon salted butter

½ cup diced white onion

½ cup bell pepper, ribs and seeds removed, diced

1 store-bought deep-dish 9-inch (23 cm) pie crust sheet

6 large eggs

1 tablespoon sour cream

½ cup freshly shredded mozzarella

¼ cup heavy cream

Salt and freshly ground black pepper, to taste

2 tablespoons chopped dill

2 tablespoons chopped parsley

8 raw large shrimp, peeled and deveined, cut into thirds

Special Equipment

9-inch (23 cm) pie dish (see Note)

High-powered blender

1. Preheat the oven to 350°F (180°C).

2. In a large frying pan set over medium heat, melt the butter. Add the onions and peppers and cook for about 10 minutes, until tender and golden brown. Set aside.

3. Fit the crust into a 9-inch (23 cm) pie dish. Prick the crust with a fork. Bake for about 8 minutes. Let cool completely.

4. In a high-powered blender, add the eggs, sour cream, mozzarella, heavy cream, salt, and pepper. Blend for at least 2 minutes until smooth and creamy. Stir in the dill and parsley until combined.

5. In the bottom of the pie crust, arrange the shrimp, onions, and peppers in an even layer. Top with the egg and cheese mixture. Season with black pepper.

6. Bake for 35 to 40 minutes until the mixture is firm and golden brown.

7. Cool for 20 minutes before serving.

Note

- A store-bought pie crust that is sold in the pan/tin/dish is an easy alternative.

SERVES	PREP	COOK	TOTAL
4	30 minutes	5 minutes	35 minutes

Pineapple Mango Shrimp Salad

Every time I make this salad it automatically makes me feel like I am sitting poolside with a spicy margarita in hand. This dish makes for a perfect dip when company comes over or even as the main event for those craving something vibrant and refreshing. The sweet heat from the dressing ties everything together; this will for sure be in your weekly rotation.

- 1 cup white wine
- 1 cup orange juice
- 1 sprig fresh rosemary
- 1 tablespoon Old Bay seasoning
- 4 garlic cloves, divided
- 1 pound (454 g) colossal shrimp, peeled and deveined
- 2 tablespoons extra-virgin olive oil
- Juice of 2 limes (about ¼ cup)
- 2 teaspoons hot honey (can substitute with regular honey to reduce heat)
- Salt and freshly ground black pepper, to taste
- 1 jalapeño pepper, ribs and seeds removed, diced
- 1 cup pineapple, ¾-inch (2 cm) dice
- 1 cup cubed mango
- 1 avocado, cubed
- ¼ cup diced red onion
- ¼ cup chopped cilantro

1. In a medium saucepan over medium heat, add the wine, orange juice, 1 cup water, rosemary, Old Bay seasoning, and 2 garlic cloves. Bring up to a boil, about 8 minutes.

2. Add the shrimp and cook for 5 minutes. Once cooked, remove the shrimp and transfer to a plate. Cover and let cool in the fridge.

3. In a large mixing bowl, whisk together the olive oil, lime juice, hot honey, salt, and pepper until smooth.

4. Cut each shrimp into three pieces. Add the shrimp, jalapeño pepper, pineapple, mango, avocado, red onion, and cilantro to the dressing and toss to combine. Serve immediately.

Notes

- You can use precooked shrimp and skip the poaching process if that's all you have on hand or to make the recipe go even quicker.
- Save the poaching liquid for a seafood bisque in the future! Strain and cool before placing into a freezer bag. Make sure to label it.
- This salad keeps for up to 2 days in the fridge but is best enjoyed immediately. Serve with freshly fried wonton wrappers, tostones, or over a bed of thinly sliced cabbage. This adds another great layer of texture, and the salad dresses it perfectly.

SERVES	PREP	COOK	TOTAL
8	10 minutes	30 minutes	40 minutes

Orange Marmalade Baked Brie

I am such a huge fan of any baked cheese. This is a great recipe if you're having people over or if you're invited over! You could put the whole thing together in advance and just bake it before serving. Use any jam/marmalade you love and whatever dough you have on hand, such as pie crust, pizza dough, or even a can of biscuits. No matter what, this recipe will be equally delicious.

- 4 sheets phyllo dough, thawed
- 3 tablespoons melted salted butter
- ½ cup orange marmalade, divided
- ½ cup crushed glazed walnuts, divided
- 1x 16-ounce (454 g) Brie wheel
- 2 Granny Smith apples, sliced
- Juice of ½ lemon

Special Equipment

Pastry brush

Parchment paper

1. Preheat the oven to 375°F (190°C).
2. Lay one sheet of phyllo dough on a sheet of parchment paper. Generously brush the dough with butter. Repeat with the remaining dough, stacking each sheet on top of one another. Add ¼ cup of marmalade and ¼ cup glazed walnuts to the middle of the dough.
3. Place the Brie on top, then cover with the remaining marmalade and nuts.
4. Brush the edges of the dough with the remaining butter.
5. To wrap the Brie, pick up each corner of the dough and cover the cheese, creating overlapping layers as needed.
6. Place the wrapped Brie seam side-down on a baking sheet.
7. Bake for about 30 minutes, until the phyllo is nice and golden.
8. **Meanwhile, prepare the apples:** Toss the sliced apples with lemon juice, then place them on a paper towel to dry.
9. To serve, cut the wrapped Brie into cubes or slice the top off and dig in with the apple slices like a dip.

Note

- I prefer to slice the white rind off the top and bottom of the wheel of Brie before baking.

MAKES	PREP	COOK	TOTAL
About 26 cookies	20 minutes (plus 30 minutes chilling time)	20 to 25 minutes	1 hour 10 minutes

Savory Thumbprint Cookies

These cookies make for a delicious and impressive appetizer. They really are such a unique twist on the classic sweet version. The combination of cheddar and fresh herbs ensures that these cookies are crunchy on the outside but perfectly moist on the inside. The possibilities in flavor combinations are endless so don't be afraid to experiment.

1 cup (16 tablespoons) salted butter, room temperature

1 egg yolk

1 cup shredded cheddar (see Notes)

¼ cup grated Pecorino Romano

2¼ cups all-purpose flour

1 teaspoon minced chives

1 teaspoon chopped parsley

¼ teaspoon salt

½ teaspoon freshly ground black pepper

1 cup prepared red pepper jelly, divided

Special Equipment

Stand mixer

Small cookie scoop (#50)

1. Line a baking sheet with parchment paper. In the bowl of a stand mixer fitted with the paddle attachment, cream the butter and egg yolk for about 3 minutes until smooth. Add the cheddar and Pecorino Romano and mix for 1 minute.

2. Add the flour, chives, parsley, salt, and pepper. Mix until the dough just comes together.

3. Use a small cookie scoop (#50; 1½ tablespoons) to form balls 1.5-inch (4 cm) in size and arrange on the baking sheet.

4. Use the end of a spoon to create a well in the middle of each cookie.

5. Scoop about 1 teaspoon of red pepper jelly into each well of the cookies. Chill the cookies in the fridge for at least 30 minutes before baking.

6. Preheat the oven to 350°F (180°C).

7. Bake for 20 to 25 minutes until the edges are lightly golden brown.

Notes

- I recommend Kerrygold Dubliner for the cheddar.
- Additional options for fillings: fig jam, honey goat cheese, sun-dried peppers, our Confit Cherry Tomato Relish (see page 57).

SERVES	PREP	COOK	TOTAL
4	10 minutes	12 minutes	22 minutes

Blue Cheese and Pecan-Stuffed Dates

This appetizer hits all the notes! Sweet, salty, creamy, and a little spicy. I am a huge fan of dates because they have such an insane natural sweetness. They taste like caramel, and they complement a stinky cheese very nicely. I add salted pecans and bacon for even more flavor and texture.

12 Medjool dates, pitted and halved

¼ cup blue cheese, preferably a wedge instead of crumbles

12 salted pecans

6 bacon slices, halved lengthwise

Hot honey, for garnish

1. Preheat the oven to 425°F (220°C). Line a large baking sheet with parchment paper.

2. Stuff each date with about 1 teaspoon blue cheese.

3. Add a whole pecan to each date. Wrap each date with a strip of bacon and arrange on the prepared baking sheet with the bacon seam side-down.

4. Bake for 10 to 12 minutes until the bacon is crispy and the cheese is melted. Drizzle with hot honey and serve warm.

Note

- Don't be discouraged if you don't love blue cheese! For a milder flavor, use goat cheese, cream cheese, or even Brie.

SERVES	PREP	COOK	TOTAL
6	5 minutes	30 minutes	35 minutes

Marinated Roasted Bread Cheese

Have you ever had bread cheese? It reminds me of cheese curds—very squeaky and doesn't melt. The outside gets crispy and the inside remains a solid cheese. The freshness from the tomato and the acid from the peppers really cuts through the fattiness of the cheese. All you need is a nice piece of bread—trust me this will be your new go-to dish when hosting. Think of it as a new age take on bruschetta but hot and cheesy!

10 ounces (283 g) cubed bread cheese

1x 10-ounce (283 g) container cherry tomatoes

8 piquante peppers, halved

¼ cup chopped parsley

3 garlic cloves, minced

¼ cup balsamic vinegar

4 tablespoons extra-virgin olive oil, divided

1 loaf Italian bread, sliced into crostini

Salt and freshly ground black pepper, to taste

Special Equipment

7 x 11-inch (18 x 28 cm) baking dish

1. Preheat the oven to 425°F (220°C).

2. In a 7 x 11-inch (18 x 28 cm) baking dish, combine the bread cheese, cherry tomatoes, piquante peppers, parsley, garlic, balsamic vinegar, and 2 tablespoons olive oil. Set aside.

3. Arrange the sliced bread on a baking sheet and drizzle with the remaining olive oil. Season with salt and pepper to taste.

4. Place the bread cheese and the crostini on separate racks in the oven. Bake the crostini for 10 to 12 minutes, rotating halfway through.

5. Meanwhile, bake the bread cheese for 25 to 30 minutes until golden brown and bubbly. (Remember: This cheese will not melt! The tomatoes and the peppers will combine like a spread.)

6. Serve these together as a warm appetizer plate and thank me later.

Note

- You can use pepper drops or peppadews in place of the piquante peppers.

MAKES
24 peppers
(6 to 8 servings)

PREP
20 minutes
(plus 15 minutes to 1 hour to marinate)

TOTAL
35 minutes to 1 hour 20 minutes

Stuffed Cherry Peppers

A friend made a version of these for me years ago and it awakened a whole new world to me. Why are we not stuffing cherry peppers more often? My version features tangy pickled cherry peppers (hot or sweet!), creamy cheese, salty prosciutto, and fresh herbs. Bite-size and bursting with flavor, they're sure to be a crowd-pleaser.

½ pound prosciutto di Parma, ½-inch (1.25 cm) dice

¼ pound sharp provolone, ½-inch (1.25 cm) dice

¼ pound Manchego, ½-inch (1.25 cm) dice

1 tablespoon chopped parsley

1 tablespoon chopped basil

1 garlic clove, grated

2 tablespoons extra-virgin olive oil

1 tablespoon red wine vinegar (or light vinegar of your choice)

Freshly ground black pepper, to taste

24 pickled cherry peppers, stems removed and hollowed; rinsed and patted dry

2 cups fresh arugula

Balsamic glaze, for garnish (about 2 tablespoons)

1. In a large bowl, combine the prosciutto, provolone, Manchego, parsley, basil, garlic, olive oil, and vinegar. Season to taste with pepper.

2. Stuff about 1 tablespoon of filling in each cherry pepper. Arrange on a platter and chill for at least 15 minutes or up to 1 hour to marinate.

3. Serve over a bed of arugula and drizzle with balsamic glaze.

Note

- You can use hot or sweet pickled peppers, depending on your heat preference.

Pasta

SERVES	PREP	COOK	TOTAL
6	20 minutes	1 hour 15 minutes	1 hour 35 minutes

Anelletti-O's

When I was growing up, my mom made pretty much everything from scratch—even our snacks! Back then, it wasn't so much about the ingredients for her. It was cheaper for her to cook our food than it was to buy the prepackaged stuff. I used to see some of my friends eating canned SpaghettiOs and I always wanted to try it. It's kind of like you want what you can't have, you know?

This homemade version of the childhood classic is packed with nostalgic flavor but made with real ingredients—perfect for when you want comfort food with a grown-up twist. A huge bonus—kids LOVE it!

For the mini meatballs

1 pound (454 g) ground beef

½ cup Italian-seasoned breadcrumbs

¼ cup grated Pecorino Romano

3 garlic cloves, minced

½ teaspoon dried oregano

½ teaspoon dried parsley

1 teaspoon onion powder

Salt and freshly ground black pepper, to taste

2 tablespoons extra-virgin olive oil

For the sauce

4 tablespoons salted butter

1 small white onion, finely diced

6 ounces (170 g) tomato paste

2x 14-ounce (397 g) cans cherry tomatoes

3 garlic cloves, minced

1 tablespoon granulated sugar

1 teaspoon garlic powder

1 teaspoon onion powder

1 teaspoon dried oregano

1 teaspoon dried parsley

1 teaspoon dried basil

Salt and freshly ground black pepper, to taste

1 pound (454 g) anelletti

¼ cup grated Pecorino Romano, plus more for garnish (optional)

Basil leaves, torn, for garnish (optional)

Crushed red pepper flakes, for garnish (optional)

1. Preheat the oven to 425°F (220°C). Line a baking sheet with parchment paper.

2. Make the mini meatballs: In a large bowl, mix the ground beef, breadcrumbs, Pecorino Romano, garlic, oregano, parsley, onion powder, salt, and pepper.

3. Roll into ½ tablespoon-sized meatballs. Arrange in an even layer on the prepared baking sheet. Drizzle with the olive oil. Toss gently to coat. Bake for 15 minutes, shaking the pan once during cooking.

4. Make the sauce: Melt the butter in a large skillet set over medium heat. Add the onion and cook for about 8 minutes until translucent.

5. Add the tomato paste and cook for about 8 minutes, stirring frequently.

6. Add the cherry tomatoes, 1 can water, the garlic, sugar, garlic powder, onion powder, oregano, parsley, basil, salt, and pepper. Bring up to a simmer, then cover and reduce the heat to low. Cook for 20 minutes, stirring occasionally.

7. Add the cooked meatballs, cover, and cook for 10 to 12 minutes.

8. Meanwhile, cook the pasta. Bring a large pot of salted water to a boil. Cook the pasta until just shy of al dente, according to package instructions. Drain.

9. Add the pasta and grated Pecorino Romano to the sauce.

10. Now this is optional, but I always add in some fresh basil at the end to just brighten it all up, a little extra grated cheese, and of course, some crushed red pepper. Serve this in a bowl and enjoy it with a spoon. This is going to be your kid's new favorite meal—you're welcome!

SERVES	PREP	COOK	TOTAL
4 to 6	15 minutes	15 minutes	30 minutes

Angel Hair Pasta with Anchovies

I am going to tell you something—anchovies really get a bad reputation. But tin fish will always be a staple in my home! The simplicity of this dish makes it easy enough for a weeknight, and the flavor is out of this world. When I was little, we used to eat this during Lent and Christmas Eve—and referred to it as "hair pasta." As an adult, that doesn't sound so appetizing. The flavor combination from the anchovies and toasted garlic will make your taste buds go wild, and that crispy topping just ties it all together. Even if you dislike anchovies, I can bet you'll love this dish.

- Salt, for pasta water
- 1 pound (454 g) angel hair pasta
- 4 tablespoons extra-virgin olive oil, divided
- ½ cup breadcrumbs
- 2x 2-ounce cans (57 g) anchovy fillets, drained
- 10 garlic cloves, thinly sliced
- Zest and juice of 1 lemon, divided
- ½ cup chopped parsley
- Grated Pecorino Romano, for garnish (optional)
- Crushed red pepper flakes, for garnish (optional)

1. Bring a large pot of water to a boil. Add salt once boiling. Cook the pasta until just shy of al dente. Reserve 1 cup pasta water.

2. Meanwhile, make the sauce: In a large skillet set over medium heat, add 2 tablespoons olive oil and the breadcrumbs. Cook for 5 to 8 minutes, stirring frequently. Set aside.

3. Heat the remaining 2 tablespoons olive oil in a 5-quart saucepan set over medium heat. Add the anchovies and garlic. Cook for about 3 minutes until the anchovies have melted into the oil and the garlic is golden. Add the lemon juice. Stir.

4. Add the cooked pasta and toss to combine. Cook for about 2 minutes until the sauce coats the noodles, adding the reserved pasta water as needed.

5. Add the lemon zest and parsley. Toss. Garnish with the breadcrumbs; add the Pecorino Romano and red pepper flakes, if using.

SERVES	PREP	COOK	TOTAL
4 to 6	10 minutes	50 minutes	1 hour

Capellini with Clam Sauce

This dish is not only delicious but SO EASY to make. I am sure you have seen this dish elsewhere but let me show you the ultimate way to make it. The marriage of the briny clams and sautéed garlic is the star of the show here. If you have any pasta dish under your belt, let it be this one.

- 1 pound (454 g) capellini
- 3 tablespoons extra-virgin olive oil, divided
- ½ cup seasoned breadcrumbs
- 8 ounces (227 g) diced pancetta
- 1 small shallot, diced (about 2 tablespoons)
- 8 garlic cloves, thinly sliced
- Salt and freshly ground pepper, to taste
- ½ cup white wine
- 3 tablespoons fresh lemon juice
- 4x 10-ounce (283 g) cans whole clams
- 1 tablespoon lemon zest
- 3 tablespoons chopped parsley
- Crushed red pepper flakes, for garnish
- Grated Pecorino Romano, for garnish

Special Equipment

Slotted spoon

1. Line a plate with paper towel. Bring a large pot of salted water to a boil. Cook the pasta until just shy of al dente.

2. In a large skillet set over medium heat, add 2 tablespoons of extra-virgin olive oil.

3. Add the breadcrumbs and toast for 3 to 5 minutes until browned, stirring often. Remove from the heat and set aside.

4. In a large skillet, add the remaining 1 tablespoon olive oil and the pancetta. Cook for about 5 minutes until crispy. Use a slotted spoon to transfer the pancetta to the prepared plate.

5. In the same skillet, add the shallot and garlic. Cook for 3 to 5 minutes until golden brown. Season to taste with salt and pepper. Add the wine and lemon juice.

6. Stir to combine and deglaze the pan. Cook the alcohol off for a few minutes until the mixture reduces by half, about 5 minutes.

7. Add the clams and simmer for about 20 minutes.

8. Add the cooked pasta, lemon zest, and chopped parsley. Toss.

9. Garnish with breadcrumbs, pancetta, red pepper flakes, and Pecorino Romano.

SERVES	PREP	COOK	TOTAL
6	10 minutes	15 minutes	25 minutes

Creamy Basil and Parsley Pesto

This recipe is great in the summer for utilizing those sun-kissed herbs! I am a huge fan of regular pesto but add a pop of parsley and I'm there even more. The splash of cream at the end really ties all the earthy herbs together. You could use any pasta shape, but I like fusilli. The sauce sits between those layers of the spiral. You are trying to stay away from pasta? This pesto can also be tossed with spaghetti squash, spread on sandwiches, or drizzled over roasted veggies!

1 pound (454 g) fusilli

½ cup plus 1 tablespoon extra-virgin olive oil

¼ cup pine nuts

3 cups fresh basil

1 cup fresh parsley

4 garlic cloves

½ cup grated Pecorino Romano, plus more for garnish

Salt and freshly ground black pepper, to taste

¼ cup heavy cream

Zest of 1 lemon, for garnish

Crushed red pepper flakes, for garnish

Special Equipment

Food processor

1. Bring a large pot of salted water to a boil. Cook the fusilli according to the package instructions. Drain and place the pasta back in the pot.

2. Heat 1 tablespoon olive oil in a small skillet set over medium heat. Add the pine nuts. Cook for 3 to 5 minutes, tossing frequently, until golden brown. Set aside.

3. In the bowl of a food processor fitted with the blade attachment, add the basil, parsley, pine nuts, garlic, Pecorino Romano, salt, and pepper. Pulse until the mixture just begins to come together. With the food processor running on low, slowly drizzle in ½ cup olive oil. Set aside.

4. Pour the pesto and heavy cream over the fusilli.

5. Stir to coat and the residual heat from the pan will pull this pasta dish together. You really don't want to put this over the stove anymore because the herbs will darken, and you want this to be a light and fresh pasta.

6. I like to serve it up with some grated Pecorino Romano and fresh lemon zest. A little crushed red pepper never hurt anybody, either. If you're not feeling pasta today, make this pesto for sandwiches, pizzas, or even drizzled on raw, fresh vegetables.

SERVES	PREP	COOK	TOTAL
6	10 minutes	55 minutes	1 hour 5 minutes

Farfalle with Roasted Shallots, Cauliflower, and Walnuts

This simple pasta dish is the perfect balance of sweet and nutty flavors. It's proof that you can create something spectacular out of nothing! It's also affordable—and you know pasta goes a long way! There are just a handful of ingredients, but they really speak for themselves. This whole meal comes together in about 30 minutes, which makes it perfect for a weeknight dinner. If you're not a fan of walnuts, then switch them out for pistachios or pine nuts—they're equally delicious!

1 pound (454 g) farfalle

1 whole head of cauliflower (about 5 cups)

6 small shallots, peeled and halved

½ cup plus 1 tablespoon extra-virgin olive oil, divided

Salt and freshly ground black pepper, to taste

½ cup roughly chopped walnuts

6 garlic cloves, chopped

Zest and juice of 1 lemon, divided

½ cup vegetable stock

3 tablespoons capers

¼ cup grated Pecorino Romano, plus more for serving

¼ cup chopped parsley

Crushed red pepper flakes, for garnish (optional)

1. Preheat the oven to 425°F (220°C).

2. Bring a large pot of salted water to a boil. Add the pasta and cook until just shy of al dente, according to package instructions. Reserve 1 cup pasta water. Drain.

3. De-core your cauliflower and cut into florets. Keep in mind that we want everything to be roughly around the same size to get the perfect bite every time. Cut these florets small like the size of the farfalle. Add to a baking sheet.

4. Add the shallots to the same baking sheet.

5. Pour ¼ cup of olive oil over the cauliflower and shallots. Season with salt and pepper. Toss to coat and place in the oven for 22 to 25 minutes, tossing halfway through.

6. Heat 1 tablespoon olive oil in a large skillet over medium heat. Add the walnuts. Cook for 3 to 5 minutes until they have browned and smell nutty. Remove from the heat and set aside.

7. Put the remaining 3 tablespoons olive oil in a large skillet set over medium heat. Add the garlic and cook for 2 to 3 minutes until fragrant.

8. Add the lemon juice and vegetable stock. Stir.

9. Sprinkle in the capers, salt, and pepper to taste. Cook for 5 to 7 minutes until thickened.

10. Add the cooked pasta, roasted cauliflower and shallots, lemon zest, remaining tablespoon of olive oil, toasted walnuts, Pecorino Romano, and parsley. Toss.

11. Cook for 2 minutes. Add the pasta water, 2 tablespoons at a time, until you reach your desired consistency.

12. At this point all that's left to do is eat it! You know I love to top mine with some crushed red pepper flakes and a little extra grated cheese. Remember this dish when your vegetarian friend is over—you'll WOW them with this delicious bowl of farfalle.

SERVES	PREP	COOK	TOTAL
8	15 minutes	1 hour 10 minutes	1 hour 25 minutes

Garden Fresh Pasta

Just because this rigatoni dish is perfect with summer vegetables does not mean we can't make it all winter. Because we are using fresh tomatoes here, the sauce does not need a long time to cook. This alone makes it a great option to keep in our weekly rotation. I love using cherry tomatoes because they have such a natural sweetness, and they make for a very tasty sauce. The nutty eggplant and salty ricotta salata tie this whole meal together. This dish is proof that simple is best!

2 eggplants, peeled and cubed (about 8 cups)

Salt and freshly ground black pepper, to taste

1 pound (454 g) rigatoni

¾ cup extra-virgin olive oil, divided

1 small yellow onion, diced (about 1 cup)

5 garlic cloves, thinly sliced

¼ cup red wine

1 pound (454 g) halved cherry tomatoes

½ cup chopped parsley

8 basil leaves, torn

1 cup grated ricotta salata

Crushed red pepper flakes, for garnish (optional)

1. Preheat the oven to 425°F (220°C). Line a baking sheet with paper towel.

2. Arrange the eggplant in an even layer on the prepared baking sheet. Salt both sides and let it rest for 15 minutes to sweat.

3. Discard the paper towel and pour ½ cup of olive oil all over the eggplant. Toss to combine.

4. Bake for 15 minutes, flipping halfway, until golden brown.

5. Bring a large pot of salted water to boil. Cook the rigatoni until just shy of al dente, according to package instructions. Reserve 1 cup of pasta water.

6. Heat the remaining ¼ cup olive oil in a 12-inch (30 cm) skillet set over medium heat.

7. Add the onion, garlic, salt, and pepper. Cook for about 12 minutes until translucent and fragrant.

8. Pour in the red wine. Cook for about 10 minutes until reduced by half.

9. Add the cherry tomatoes and cook for about 20 minutes until they break down.

10. Then add the rigatoni, roasted eggplant, parsley, basil, and ricotta salata. Toss to combine, adding a splash of pasta water as needed. Garnish with red pepper flakes, if desired.

Note

- If you don't like eggplant, this dish is also SO GOOD with zucchini and summer squash. Same exact process, just switch out the vegetables.

SERVES	PREP	COOK	TOTAL
6	20 minutes	55 minutes	1 hour 15 minutes

Pasta con le Sarde

Every March, around St. Joseph's Day, I would look forward to a nice bowl of Pasta con le Sarde. This classic Sicilian dish is loaded with fennel, sardines, and raisins. . . did I lose you? When my grandpa passed, my grandma and I were the only two people in the house that still enjoyed it. I will never forget us going to the store together to pick up the can of Cuoco Seasoning—it was like our little tradition. When she passed, I made a point to still make it and, of course, put my own little fresh twist on it. This dish is proof that food is the center of everything. Even just the smell of this simmering will send me right back to her little kitchen in Glendale, Queens, overlooking the cemetery.

6 tablespoons extra-virgin olive oil, divided

1 cup Italian-seasoned breadcrumbs

¼ cup pine nuts

1 small yellow onion, diced (about ½ cup)

1 fennel bulb, thinly sliced (about 1 cup)

Salt and freshly ground black pepper, to taste

1x 14½-ounce (411 g) can of Cuoco Seasoning for Macaroni with Sardines

1x 28-ounce (794 g) can whole peeled tomatoes

6 garlic cloves, thinly sliced

1 pound (454 g) bucatini

¼ cup golden raisins

2 tablespoons chopped parsley

2 tablespoons chopped basil

Grated Pecorino Romano, for garnish (optional)

Crushed red pepper flakes, for garnish (optional)

1. Heat 3 tablespoons olive oil in a large 9-inch (23 cm) frying pan set over medium heat and add the breadcrumbs. Cook for about 5 minutes, tossing frequently. Transfer to a plate and set aside.

2. Now let's toast our pine nuts for later. Add 1 tablespoon olive oil in the same frying pan. Add the pine nuts and cook for 3 to 5 minutes, stirring frequently. Transfer to a plate and set aside.

3. In a large pot set over medium heat, heat the remaining 2 tablespoons olive oil. Add the onions and fennel. Season to taste with salt. Cook for about 10 minutes, stirring occasionally.

4. Add the Cuoco Seasoning, tomatoes, garlic, salt, and pepper. Stir. Bring to a light simmer, then reduce the heat to medium-low and cover. Cook for 20 minutes.

5. Bring a large pot of salted water to a boil. Add the bucatini and cook until just shy of al dente.

6. Reserve 1 cup of pasta water. Drain and add the pasta to the tomato sauce.

7. Add the toasted pine nuts, golden raisins, and 3 tablespoons toasted breadcrumbs. Cook for about 2 minutes until thickened. Add a splash of pasta water and toss until you reach your desired consistency. Add the parsley and basil and toss again.

8. Garnish with breadcrumbs, and the Pecorino Romano and red pepper flakes, if desired.

SERVES	PREP	COOK	TOTAL
6	5 minutes	45 minutes	50 minutes

Rigatoni with Sausage and Peas

A comforting, hearty pasta dish packed with peas and sausage, this is perfect for a weeknight dinner or a cozy gathering. With just a handful of ingredients this meal comes together so quickly, and I bet you have all the ingredients on hand. This meal is so satisfying, and it screams childhood to me. Don't like peas? Swap them out for broccoli or cauliflower! I love to serve this dish with red pepper flakes for heat and some crusty bread.

- 1 pound (454 g) rigatoni
- 4 tablespoons extra-virgin olive oil, divided
- 1 pound (454 g) sweet Italian sausage meat, removed from the casing
- 1 medium yellow onion, diced (about 1 cup)
- 6 garlic cloves, thinly sliced
- ½ cup chicken stock
- Salt and freshly ground black pepper, to taste
- 1x 16-ounce (454 g) bag thawed frozen peas
- ½ cup grated Pecorino Romano
- 2 tablespoons chopped parsley
- Crushed red pepper flakes (optional)

1. Line a plate with paper towel. Bring a large pot of salted water to a boil. Cook the pasta just shy of al dente, according to package instructions. Reserve 1 cup of pasta water. Drain.

2. Heat 2 tablespoons olive oil in a 5-quart saucepan set over medium heat. Add the sausage and cook for about 8 minutes until golden brown. Transfer to the prepared plate and set aside.

3. In the same pan, add 1 tablespoon olive oil and the onions. Cook for about 12 minutes until translucent.

4. Add the sausage, garlic, and stock and bring up to a simmer, about 10 minutes. Season to taste with salt and pepper.

5. Add the peas and cook for about 3 minutes. Remove from the heat.

6. Add the cooked pasta, remaining tablespoon of olive oil, the Pecorino Romano, and parsley.

7. Toss to combine, adding pasta water as necessary until you reach your desired consistency. Garnish with red pepper flakes, if desired.

SERVES	PREP	COOK	TOTAL
6	10 minutes	1 hour 10 minutes	1 hour 20 minutes

Sherry Cherry Tomato Sauce with Shrimp

This is another recipe we LOVE to cook in the summer with all those garden tomatoes. The sauce is similar to a marinara, but it includes some sautéed fennel, which really transforms the whole sauce. I love to serve this over gemelli, but it can also be served with some crusty bread and used as an appetizer.

3 tablespoons extra-virgin olive oil, divided

1 small yellow onion, thinly sliced (about ½ cup)

1 fennel bulb, thinly sliced

Salt and freshly ground black pepper, to taste

2x 10-ounce (283 g) containers cherry tomatoes, halved

4 garlic cloves, thinly sliced

½ cup dry sherry

1 pound (454 g) gemelli

1 pound (454 g) large shrimp, peeled and deveined

½ cup grated Pecorino Romano, for garnish

6 basil leaves, torn, for garnish

Crushed red pepper flakes, for garnish (optional)

1. Bring a large pot of salted water to a boil.

2. Heat 2 tablespoons oil in a large skillet set over medium heat. Add the onion and fennel. Cook for 8 to 10 minutes until softened. Season to taste with salt and pepper.

3. Then add the cherry tomatoes. Cook for about 10 minutes, until the tomatoes have broken down.

4. Add the garlic. Cook for about 3 minutes.

5. Pour the sherry in the pan, lower the heat to medium-low, and cook for about 30 minutes until the mixture has reduced by half.

6. Meanwhile, cook the pasta according to the package instructions. Drain and set aside.

7. Add the shrimp to the tomato mixture. Cook for 5 to 7 minutes, until the shrimp are opaque.

8. Transfer the cooked pasta to a large serving bowl. Top with the tomato and shrimp mixture. Garnish with the remaining tablespoon of olive oil, Pecorino Romano, basil, and red pepper flakes, if using.

Note

- This recipe is great because you could really use any shellfish here. It even works well with a can of scungilli or mussels!

SERVES	PREP	COOK	TOTAL
4 to 6	10 minutes	35 minutes (plus 20 minutes resting time)	1 hour 5 minutes

Spaghetti Pie

I can't be the only one who makes way too much spaghetti when cooking dinner. Maybe subconsciously I know we can always just make a delicious spaghetti pie. I mean, those crispy bits are life-changing. This recipe combines the comfort of spaghetti with the hardiness of a baked casserole. Plus, it's a great way to use up leftovers!

2 tablespoons extra-virgin olive oil, divided

2 tablespoons seasoned breadcrumbs, divided

½ pound (227 g) cooked spaghetti

2 large eggs

2 tablespoons ricotta

2 tablespoons grated Pecorino Romano

½ cup shredded mozzarella

2 garlic cloves, finely minced

1 tablespoon chopped parsley

Salt and freshly ground black pepper, to taste

Special Equipment

11-inch (28 cm) springform pan

Pastry brush

1. Preheat the oven to 375°F (190°C). Brush an 11-inch (28 cm) springform pan with 1 tablespoon olive oil. Spread 1 tablespoon of breadcrumbs evenly on the bottom and sides of the pan.

2. In a large bowl, mix the cooked pasta, eggs, ricotta, Pecorino Romano, mozzarella, garlic, parsley, salt, and pepper.

3. Transfer the mixture to the prepared springform pan. Drizzle the pie with the remaining tablespoon of olive oil and breadcrumbs.

4. Bake for 30 to 35 minutes. Let cool for at least 20 minutes before you try releasing it from the pan. You could serve this hot, room temperature, or even just cold from the fridge. Trust me, you'll never throw out your leftover spaghetti again.

SERVES	PREP	COOK	TOTAL
6	15 minutes	50 minutes	1 hour 5 minutes

Swordfish Pasta

When I was growing up, my grandmother cooked swordfish very often. It used to be the poor man's fish—now you can't get your hands on it without it costing $40 a pound! When I see it on sale, this is the dish that's on the menu for the night. Pour yourself a glass of wine and enjoy this Sicilian classic.

⅓ cup extra-virgin olive oil, divided

1 medium eggplant, diced

Salt and freshly ground black pepper, to taste

1 small red onion, thinly sliced

6 garlic cloves, thinly sliced

24 ounces (680 g) cherry tomatoes, halved

½ cup dry white wine, such as sauvignon blanc or pinot grigio

1 pound (454 g) bucatini

3 tablespoons capers

½ cup roughly chopped Castelvetrano olives

2 tablespoons chopped mint, plus more for serving

1½ pounds (680 g) swordfish, cut into bite-size cubes

Crushed red pepper flakes, for garnish

Grated Pecorino Romano, for garnish

1. Line a plate with paper towel. Bring a large pot of salted water to a boil.

2. Heat 2 tablespoons olive oil in a large skillet set over medium-high heat. Add the eggplant and salt. Cook for 12 minutes. Transfer to the prepared plate.

3. Add the remaining olive oil with the onion, salt, and pepper and cook for about 5 minutes until translucent.

4. Add the garlic and cherry tomatoes. Cook for 8 to 10 minutes until softened and jammy.

5. Deglaze the pan with white wine, scraping up anything from the bottom of your pan. Simmer for 4 to 5 minutes until reduced slightly.

6. Meanwhile, cook the bucatini until just shy of al dente. Reserve ½ cup pasta water.

7. Add the capers, olives, and mint to the tomato mixture. Cook for about 2 minutes.

8. Add the swordfish to the cherry tomato mixture. Cook for 5 to 6 minutes.

9. Add the eggplant. Stir. Remove from the heat.

10. In a large serving bowl, add the bucatini. Pour the sauce and swordfish over the pasta. Garnish with fresh mint, red pepper flakes, and if you are feeling like a rebel, even a little grated Pecorino Romano. Blasphemy, I know. I didn't need any reserved pasta liquid, but if you feel yours isn't saucy enough, splash a little bit in throughout the tossing process. And make sure you DM me after you make this one to let me know how long you've been sleeping on swordfish.

SERVES	PREP	COOK	TOTAL
6 to 8	20 minutes (plus 4+ hours to marinate)	10 minutes	4 hours 30 minutes

The Ultimate Tortellini Salad

This tortellini salad is a great way to use up leftover antipasto from the night before. It is also great after it marinates in the fridge for a day or two, which makes it perfect for hosting or meal prep. It features cheese tortellini, cured meats, and pickled veggies—all dressed in a homemade vinaigrette. The best part about this recipe is that it's highly customizable! This is my classic combination, but you can use whatever you have in the house.

12 ounces (340 g) cheese tortellini

¼ cup halved black olives

¼ cup halved mozzarella balls

¼ cup diced Genoa salami

¼ cup prosciutto, cut into bite-size pieces

¼ cup sliced roasted red peppers

¼ cup chopped pickled giardiniera

¼ cup sliced sun-dried tomatoes in oil

¼ cup diced cucumber

¼ cup thinly sliced red onion

2 garlic cloves, minced

2 tablespoons chopped parsley

2 tablespoons chopped basil

¼ cup extra-virgin olive oil

¼ cup red wine vinegar

½ teaspoon dried oregano

Salt and freshly ground black pepper, to taste

1. Bring a large pot of salted water to a boil. Cook the tortellini according to package instructions. Drain. Set aside to cool.

2. In a large bowl, mix the olives, mozzarella, salami, prosciutto, red peppers, giardiniera, sun-dried tomatoes, cucumber, red onion, and garlic.

3. Add the drained and cooled cheese tortellini, parsley, basil, olive oil, red wine vinegar, and oregano. Toss. Season to taste with salt and pepper.

4. You can serve immediately but it tastes even better if you can marinate it for at least 4 hours. The longer the better!

Sides

SERVES
6

COOK
40 minutes

TOTAL
40 minutes

Brown Butter Polenta

If you are tired of mashed potatoes, this one's for you! What is more comforting than browned butter and sage? This duo pairs beautifully with roasted meats like chicken or short ribs, mushrooms, or even just a poached egg for a cozy brunch. Just the smell of this cooking on the stove will put you in a good mood.

6 tablespoons salted butter

12 sage leaves

2 cups whole milk

2 teaspoons salt

1 cup coarse cornmeal

1 cup grated Pecorino Romano

Freshly ground black pepper, to taste

Special Equipment

Slotted spoon

Wire rack

1. Melt the butter in a small saucepan set over medium-low heat. Cook for about 5 minutes, until it starts to smell nutty and foams on the top.

2. Add the sage leaves, working in batches as needed, and cook for 1 to 2 minutes. Use a spider or slotted spoon to transfer the sage to a paper towel or wire rack.

3. In a large pot set over high heat, add 2 cups water, the milk, and salt. Bring to a boil, about 8 minutes. Reduce the heat to low and slowly pour in the cornmeal in a steady stream, whisking constantly to prevent lumps.

4. Cook the polenta, stirring frequently with a wooden spoon for about 20 to 25 minutes, until it thickens and pulls away from the sides of the pan.

5. Add the sage-infused brown butter, Pecorino Romano, and black pepper. Taste and adjust for seasoning. Garnish with the fried sage leaves and serve.

Note

- The leftovers are really delicious when sliced into cubes and fried to create polenta croutons.

SERVES
6 to 8

PREP
15 minutes

COOK
15 minutes (plus 30 minutes resting time)

TOTAL
1 hour

Bruschetta Bread Salad

One thing I really admired about my grandmother was her ability to never waste food. This delicious salad that I grew up eating really showcases that. It's made with simple, flavorful ingredients that really speak for themselves and also utilizes stale bread.

1 loaf of semolina bread, cubed and at least one day old (about 10 inches; 25 cm long)

½ cup plus 1 tablespoon extra-virgin olive oil, divided

Salt and freshly ground black pepper, to taste

4 tablespoons balsamic vinegar

2 tablespoons balsamic glaze

4 garlic cloves, grated (about 2 tablespoons)

1 teaspoon Dijon mustard

4 tomatoes on the vine, diced (about 2 cups)

1 English cucumber, thinly sliced on the diagonal (about 2 cups)

1 red onion, thinly sliced half-moons (about 1 cup)

3 ounces (85 g) black olives, halved (about ½ cup)

8 ounces (85 g) mozzarella pearls

2 tablespoons chopped parsley

1 bunch basil leaves, torn (about ½ cup)

1. Preheat the oven to 425°F (220°C).

2. Toss the cubed bread with 1 tablespoon olive oil, salt, and pepper. Arrange in a single layer on a large baking sheet. Bake for about 15 minutes, stirring occasionally, until crisp and golden brown. Cool completely.

3. In a large bowl, whisk together the remaining olive oil, the balsamic vinegar, balsamic glaze, garlic, and mustard. Season to taste with salt and pepper.

4. Add the tomatoes, cucumbers, red onions, and olives and toss to combine.

5. Add the cooled bread cubes, mozzarella, parsley, and basil. Toss to combine.

6. Let sit for at least 30 minutes before serving.

Notes

- This can be made ahead! Do every step besides adding the toasted bread. Store your bread separately in a zip-top bag until 30 minutes before serving.
- Any bread will work! I prefer to use a nice crusty semolina bread like my Semi-Semolina Loaf (see page 158) but let's face it, this recipe is tailored to what you have in the fridge and reducing food waste.

SERVES	PREP	COOK	TOTAL
6	5 minutes	1 hour	1 hour 5 minutes

Butter Poached Garlic Mashed Potatoes

These really are the ultimate mashed potatoes. You are getting a two-for-one with this recipe! I will show you how to butter poach garlic *and* how to make the most delicious mashed potatoes of your life! They are silky, indulgent, and full of flavor. What I love about this recipe is that it's simple enough to whip up for weeknight dinners but decadent enough for your holiday table.

1 cup (16 tablespoons) salted butter

12 garlic cloves

1 sprig rosemary

2 sprigs thyme

2 pounds (907 g) Yukon Gold potatoes, peeled and halved

½ cup whole milk

½ cup heavy cream

2 tablespoons sour cream

Salt and freshly ground black pepper, to taste

1. In a small pot set over medium-low heat, add the butter, garlic, rosemary, and thyme. Cook for 20 to 25 minutes until the garlic is fork-tender.

2. In a large pot of salted water set over high heat, add the potatoes. Cook for 25 to 35 minutes until they are fork-tender. Strain and set aside.

3. Once the garlic is tender, remove the stems from the herbs and pour the butter and garlic over the cooked potatoes. Use a potato masher to break down the garlic and potatoes until you achieve your desired consistency. Add the milk, heavy cream, sour cream, salt, and pepper. Mix until just combined. Remove the herb leaves before serving.

Notes

- You can use white pepper instead of black pepper if you don't want to see the back specks in your potatoes.
- For smoother, creamier mashed potatoes, use a potato ricer rather than a traditional masher.

SERVES	PREP	COOK	TOTAL
4	10 minutes	45 minutes	55 minutes

Roasted Cauliflower Francese

She's golden, she's saucy, she's got that zesty attitude, and she could totally be more than just a side dish. I love to pair roasted cauliflower with a grilled protein for a dinner that's instantly luxurious—just like the sauce at the bottom of this cauliflower.

1 head cauliflower

½ cup (8 tablespoons) salted butter

1 small shallot, diced

4 garlic cloves, thinly sliced

Juice of 2 lemons

1 tablespoon chicken bouillon powder

1 tablespoon chopped parsley, plus more for garnish

1. Preheat the oven to 400°F (200°C).

2. Remove the outer leaves from the cauliflower. Cut off the bottom of the stem to create an even surface. Place in a large baking dish or Dutch oven and set aside.

3. In a large, microwave-safe bowl, add the butter, shallots, garlic, lemon juice, and chicken bouillon.

4. Microwave on high for about 1 minute until the butter is melted.

5. Add the parsley, and stir.

6. Pour the butter over the cauliflower, cover, and bake for about 45 minutes or until the cauliflower is fork-tender.

7. Uncover the cauliflower and broil for 2 minutes until browned. Cool for about 5 minutes before serving. To garnish, sprinkle with fresh parsley.

SERVES	PREP	COOK	TOTAL
4 to 6	10 minutes	50 minutes	1 hour

Delicata Squash Au Gratin

This recipe came to life when I had some delicata squash staring at me on the counter. I feel like squash can be intimidating because usually they're hard to cut and peel. What's great here is the peel is completely edible *and* it's packed with vitamins, so it's a win-win. This is a little different than your typical sweet potato or butternut squash gratin. My version has a nice nuttiness to it that pairs really well with cheese.

- 2 delicata squash, cleaned, halved, and cut into half moons
- 1 cup shredded Fontina
- 4 tablespoons unsalted butter
- 1 medium shallot, diced
- 3 garlic cloves, chopped
- 2 cups heavy cream
- 1 teaspoon poultry seasoning
- Salt and freshly ground black pepper, to taste
- 1 teaspoon thyme, dried or fresh
- ¼ cup Italian-seasoned breadcrumbs
- ¼ cup grated Pecorino Romano
- Chopped parsley, for garnish

1. Preheat the oven to 400°F (200°C).

2. Arrange the squash in a single layer in a baking dish. Layer the shredded Fontina on top of the squash. Set aside.

3. Melt the butter in a medium saucepan set over medium heat. Now let's sauté up the aromatics and warm up the cream. Add the shallot and cook for 3 to 5 minutes. Add the garlic and cook for about 1 minute.

4. Add the heavy cream, poultry seasoning, salt, pepper, and thyme. Stir and cook for about 5 minutes until the mixture begins to boil.

5. Pour the milk mixture over the cheese and squash. Top with breadcrumbs and Pecorino Romano.

6. Cover tightly with foil and bake for 20 minutes.

7. Remove the foil and bake for another 20 minutes until the squash is tender and golden brown. Garnish with fresh parsley and serve.

SERVES	PREP	COOK	TOTAL
4	5 minutes	5 minutes	10 minutes

Garlicky Cannellini Beans

Canned beans are super underrated. Everyone has a can in their pantry—and they are packed with fiber and protein! When you sauté cannellini beans, it really brings out their rich, nutty flavor. This recipe showcases the flavor of the beans and is the perfect hearty side dish. With just a handful of ingredients, these beans really pack a punch.

2 tablespoons extra-virgin olive oil

1x 15½-ounce (439 g) can cannellini beans, rinsed and drained

2 garlic cloves, grated

1 tablespoon chopped parsley

Salt and freshly ground black pepper, to taste

Lemon wedges (optional)

1. Heat the olive oil in a 12-inch (30 cm) skillet set over medium heat. Add the beans and cook for 4 to 5 minutes until the skin starts to peel away.

2. Remove from the heat. Add the garlic, parsley, salt, pepper, and juice from the lemon wedges, if desired, to taste. Stir.

Note

- I like to use cannellini beans, but you could use Great Northern or butter beans, too.

SERVES	PREP	COOK	TOTAL
6	15 minutes	25 minutes	40 minutes

Grandma's String Bean and Potato Salad

Growing up in my grandma's kitchen, this salad was a staple. She made it all summer long because she had string beans growing everywhere in her yard. I have such fond memories of backyard barbecues as a kid. Chicken legs and this exact salad were served easily once a week. This side dish is not only so easy to prepare but also a crowd-pleaser! It is even better as it sits, which makes it a great option for meal prep and hosting.

1 pound (454 g) trimmed string beans

2 pounds (907 g) red potatoes

¼ cup extra-virgin olive oil

2 tablespoons red wine vinegar

1 tablespoon fresh lemon juice

1 small red onion, thinly sliced

4 garlic cloves, minced

1 tablespoon chopped parsley

4 basil leaves, torn

Salt and freshly ground black pepper, to taste

Crushed red pepper flakes (optional)

1. Fill a large bowl with ice water. Set aside.

2. Bring a medium pot of water to a boil. Cook the string beans for 3 to 5 minutes. Transfer to the ice bath to stop cooking.

3. Bring a large pot of water to a boil over medium heat. Add the potatoes and cook for about 20 minutes until fork-tender.

4. In a large bowl, add the olive oil, red wine vinegar, lemon juice, red onion, and garlic. Whisk to combine.

5. Add the potatoes, string beans, parsley, and torn basil to the dressing. Season to taste with salt and pepper. Top with crushed red pepper flakes, if desired. Serve warm or at room temperature.

SERVES	PREP	COOK	TOTAL
6	15 minutes	15 minutes	30 minutes

Grilled Corn Salad with Basil Butter

This grilled corn salad is all I want on a nice summer night. It's easy, flavorful, and half of the ingredients are found in my garden. It also looks so pretty in the bowl and can be made in advance. You just pour the warm butter over it right before serving. I love making this when we do seafood boils. It's salty and sweet, which, to me, is the perfect pairing.

1 tablespoon extra-virgin olive oil

¼ cup pine nuts

6 ears of corn, husked

3 tablespoons mayonnaise

¼ cup quartered cherry tomatoes

¼ cup chopped pickled red onions

½ cup crumbled queso fresco

¼ cup torn basil leaves

5 tablespoons salted butter

2 garlic cloves, grated

1 tablespoon honey

Juice of 3 lemons (about ¾ cup)

Salt and freshly ground black pepper, to taste

2 tablespoons chopped basil

Special Equipment

Pastry brush

Grill

1. Heat the oil in a large skillet set over medium heat. Add the pine nuts and toast for 3 to 5 minutes. Set aside.

2. Brush the corn evenly with the mayonnaise. Preheat the grill. Grill the corn for about 10 minutes until evenly charred. Transfer to a large bowl and cover with plastic wrap to steam. Set aside.

3. In a large bowl, add the cherry tomatoes, red onions, queso fresco, basil, and pine nuts. Set aside.

4. Cut the corn off the cob and add to the tomato mixture.

5. In a microwave-safe bowl, combine the butter, garlic, honey, and lemon juice. Season to taste with salt and pepper.

6. Microwave for about 1 minute until the butter is melted. Add the chopped basil. Stir. Pour over the corn and tomato salad and toss to combine.

Note

- If you don't have a grill, you can cook the corn in a hot pan set over high heat on the stove or in the oven; just keep an eye on them and make sure you're turning them frequently.

SERVES	PREP	COOK	TOTAL
6	10 minutes	20 minutes	30 minutes

Lemon Herby Couscous

Couscous—the food so nice they named it twice! This is my go-to side dish when I want something light, refreshing, and full of flavor. It's easy and a perfect balance of lemon and fresh herbs. Whether you serve it on the side of grilled protein or as the base for a bowl, it's a delicious addition to any meal.

2 tablespoons salted butter

2 cups pearl couscous

3 cups chicken stock

1 tablespoon chicken bouillon powder

2 tablespoons minced garlic

Juice from 2 lemons

3 tablespoons chopped parsley

3 tablespoons chopped dill

1. Melt the butter in a 5-quart saucepan set over medium heat. Add the couscous and cook for 5 to 8 minutes, stirring frequently, until browned.

2. Add the chicken stock, chicken bouillon, and garlic. Cook, uncovered, for 10 to 12 minutes until the liquid has evaporated.

3. Remove from the heat and stir in the lemon juice. Let it cool for about 5 minutes. Add the parsley and dill. Stir. Serve immediately or at room temperature.

Note

- This side pairs so well with any protein. Some of my favorites are scallops or roasted chicken thighs.

SERVES	PREP	COOK	TOTAL
8	15 minutes (plus 1 hour resting time)	10 minutes	1 hour 25 minutes

Grilled Vegetable Salad

This is a delicious side dish that also works as an appetizer. It can be added to an antipasto board or even used as a condiment for sandwiches! The homemade salad dressing really makes this dish shine and marinates those vegetables beautifully. We eat this all summer long with our homegrown vegetables. I will make a big batch on a Sunday and incorporate it into meals all week. Most of the veggies will be sliced thin, so it's best to use a mandolin or a very sharp chef's knife.

1 zucchini, thinly sliced

1 yellow squash, thinly sliced

1 Italian eggplant, peeled and thinly sliced

1 red bell pepper, ribs and seeds removed, quartered

1 red onion, thickly sliced

2 portobello mushroom caps

Salt and freshly ground black pepper, to taste

4 garlic cloves, grated

½ cup plus 2 tablespoons extra-virgin olive oil, divided

½ cup balsamic vinegar

1 teaspoon Dijon mustard

Juice of 1 lemon (about ¼ cup)

1 tablespoon raw honey

8 basil leaves, torn

¼ cup chopped parsley

Special Equipment

Wire rack

Mason jar

Grill or cast-iron grill pan

1. Line a large baking sheet with a wire rack or paper towels. Arrange the zucchini, yellow squash, eggplant, bell pepper, red onions, and portobello mushroom caps in an even layer. Season generously with salt and rest for 1 hour to draw out the moisture.

2. In a mason jar, add the grated garlic, ½ cup olive oil, the balsamic vinegar, mustard, lemon juice, honey, basil, parsley, salt, and pepper. Seal the jar and shake until emulsified.

3. In a large bowl, combine the vegetables and 2 tablespoons olive oil. Massage until coated.

4. Preheat the grill or a cast-iron grill pan on the stove. Place the vegetables on the grill, working in batches as needed to avoid overcrowding. Cook for 3 or 4 minutes per side. Once cooked, place them in the same bowl.

5. While the vegetables are still warm, add the dressing and toss to combine.

Note

- I love eating this salad as is but my other favorite way is to make a grilled vegetable sandwich on my Semi-Semolina Loaf (see page 158). Layer the beautiful grilled vegetables, some salted fresh mozzarella, and a nice drizzle of the dressing in the bottom of the bowl and serve on the semolina bread.

SERVES	PREP	COOK	TOTAL
4	10 minutes	55 minutes	1 hour 5 minutes

Stewed Zucchini and Tomatoes

This rustic and comforting vegetable dish is not only delicious but so versatile. It works great as a side dish but can easily be turned into a full entrée. Add a can of beans, some pasta, and a piece of crusty bread—a match made in heaven. I always remember my family making this way more often in the summertime. When I saw my grandma had an abundance of tomatoes and zucchinis from the garden, I KNEW this was going to be served at dinner.

2 tablespoons extra-virgin olive oil

1 medium yellow onion, diced (about ½ cup)

6 fresh tomatoes, diced (about 3 cups)

3 medium zucchinis, diced (about 4 cups)

5 garlic cloves, minced

¼ cup chicken stock

Salt and freshly ground black pepper, to taste

2 tablespoons chopped parsley

¼ cup chopped basil

½ cup frozen peas, thawed

Crushed red pepper flakes, for garnish (optional)

Grated Pecorino Romano, for garnish (optional)

1. Heat the olive oil in a 5-quart saucepan over medium heat. Add the onion and cook for 10 to 12 minutes until translucent and fragrant.

2. Add the tomatoes and cook for 10 to 12 minutes until they break down and reduce.

3. Add the zucchini, garlic, and stock. Season to taste with salt and pepper. Cover and cook for 25 to 30 minutes.

4. Remove from the heat and stir in the parsley, basil, and peas. Garnish with red pepper flakes and Pecorino Romano, if desired. Serve warm.

Note

- You can use vegetable stock if you want to make this vegetarian-friendly.

SERVES	PREP	COOK	TOTAL
6	10 minutes	20 minutes	30 minutes

Tangy Herbed Potato Salad

This herb-infused potato salad is a fun and flavorful twist on a classic. The crispy salt-and-vinegar-chip topping just makes it the perfect bite. After all, a little potato on potato action never hurt anybody. Whether you are serving it at a summer barbecue or just enjoying it relaxing on your couch, it's sure to steal the show!

- 2 pounds (907 g) baby potatoes
- 1 cup mayonnaise
- 1 tablespoon Dijon mustard
- 1 tablespoon apple cider vinegar
- 1 tablespoon fresh lemon juice
- 1 tablespoon extra-virgin olive oil
- 2 garlic cloves, grated
- ¼ cup chopped bread-and-butter pickles
- Salt and freshly ground black pepper, to taste
- 2 tablespoons chopped parsley
- 2 tablespoons chopped dill
- 2 tablespoons chopped chives
- Kettle cooked salt and vinegar chips, for serving

1. Bring a large pot of salted water to a boil. Add the potatoes and cook for 15 to 20 minutes until they are fork-tender.

2. In a medium bowl, whisk together the mayonnaise, mustard, apple cider vinegar, lemon juice, olive oil, garlic, pickles, salt, and pepper. Chill in the fridge.

3. Strain the potatoes and set aside to cool. Dice the potatoes into 1½-inch (4 cm) pieces. Add the potatoes, parsley, dill, and chives to the dressing. Toss until combined.

4. Before serving, crush the salt and vinegar chips over the top.

SERVES	PREP	COOK	TOTAL
6	15 minutes	35 minutes	50 minutes

Unstuffed Artichokes

The recipe that broke the internet! Aren't you tired of stuffing artichokes? What a hassle—cleaning the little hairs, snipping the tips, taking forever to cook! What if I told you, there is a better way? This dish features all the amazing qualities of a stuffed artichoke in a casserole form. The result is more surface area for texture and just the artichoke hearts, which are, after all, the best part.

2x 12-ounce (340 g) bags frozen artichokes, thawed (see Note)

4 garlic cloves, minced

½ cup chopped parsley

½ cup extra-virgin olive oil

1 cup Italian-seasoned breadcrumbs

½ cup grated Pecorino Romano

1 teaspoon garlic powder

1 teaspoon onion powder

Zest and juice of 1 lemon

Salt and freshly ground black pepper, to taste

1 cup shredded mozzarella, divided

Special Equipment

9 x 13-inch (23 x 33 cm) baking dish or oval dish of similar size

1. Preheat the oven 375°F (190°C).

2. Pat the thawed artichoke hearts dry with paper towels.

3. In a large bowl, add the artichokes, garlic, parsley, olive oil, breadcrumbs, Pecorino Romano, garlic powder, onion powder, and zest and juice of 1 lemon. Season to taste with salt and pepper.

4. In a greased 9 x 13-inch (23 x 33 cm) baking dish, add in half of the artichoke mixture in an even layer. Top with half of the shredded mozzarella. Layer with the remaining artichoke mixture, followed by the remaining mozzarella.

5. Bake for 30 to 35 minutes, rotating halfway through the cooking process. Serve immediately!

Note

- It may be hard to find the artichokes in your frozen foods section. Second option for me would be the blanched artichokes in a can, not marinated. If you can only find the ones in a jar just strain off that liquid and make sure to pat dry. I would also change the cooking temperature to 400°F (200°C) and cook for about 20 minutes. Although it will still be delicious, I do feel like the texture will be different than the original recipe.

Cocktails

SERVES	PREP	TOTAL
6	5 minutes (plus 8 hours freezing and 2 hours chilling time)	10 hours 10 minutes

Sunset White Sangria

This batch cocktail is great to make in advance and is my go-to for a large gathering. It has the perfect balance of tropical flavors that makes it feel a bit more special than what it is. I make this often in the warmer months; it's great for a pool party or a nice barbecue. My trick is to freeze the fruit before serving to keep your cocktail cold.

½ cup mango chunks

½ cup pineapple chunks

1x 15-ounce (425 g) can lychees in syrup, drained, liquid reserved

½ cup pomegranate seeds

1 orange, sliced

1x (750 ml) bottle dry white wine, such as pinot grigio or sauvignon blanc

½ cup lychee liqueur

½ cup Malibu

½ cup pineapple juice

Juice of 4 mandarin oranges

Juice of 2 limes

Sparkling water, to finish

Special Equipment

Parchment paper

Pitcher

1. Line a baking sheet with parchment paper. Arrange the mango, pineapple, lychee, pomegranate seeds, and orange slices in an even layer. Freeze for at least 8 hours.

2. In a large pitcher, add the wine, reserved lychee juice, lychee liqueur, Malibu, pineapple juice, orange juice, and lime juice. Stir! Chill for at least 2 hours.

3. Add ice and a handful of the mixed frozen fruit into a red wine glass. Pour in the prepared cocktail. Top with sparkling water.

Notes

- You can use plain sparkling water, but I like something with flavor—lime, lemon, or even a strawberry seltzer would be perfect.
- If you can't find lychee liqueur, you could use Cointreau or Aperol.

SERVES	PREP	TOTAL
1	5 minutes	10 minutes

SunGold Spritzer

SunGolds are basically kiwi's hotter cousin! They have a milder skin so you can just enjoy them as is, no need to peel in this case! They are higher in natural sugar, making them way sweeter than a kiwi. Which also makes them PERFECT for a refreshing cocktail. I can find these anywhere around me, but a kiwi will work just as well for this recipe if you can't find SunGolds.

1 fresh mint sprig (about 3 leaves)

1 teaspoon granulated sugar

1 SunGold, peeled and cut into chunks

Juice of 1 lime

Juice of 1 mandarin orange

1 ounce (25 ml) vodka

4 ounces (100 ml) champagne

Special Equipment

Highball glass

Muddler

Cocktail shaker

Fine-mesh sieve

1. Place a highball glass in the freezer.
2. In a cocktail shaker (or a big mason jar with a tight lid), muddle the mint and sugar. Add the SunGolds, lime juice, and mandarin orange juice. Muddle for 1 to 2 minutes.
3. Strain the mixture through a fine-mesh sieve into a bowl.
4. Fill the cocktail shaker with ice. Add the SunGold mixture and vodka. Place the lid on the shaker and shake vigorously until cold.
5. Fill the chilled highball glass with ice. Strain the cocktail into the glass and top with champagne.

Note

- You can omit the vodka and champagne to make this a mocktail.

SERVES	PREP	TOTAL
1	5 minutes	10 minutes

Strawberry Basil Aperol Spritz

Does anyone even actually like an Aperol Spritz? Or do we just like the concept of it? My take on it is fruity and garden fresh. Plus, it utilizes all the mint I have growing in my yard. It's perfect for a date with your girlfriends! Everyone needs a good cocktail and yap session.

2 basil leaves

1 ounce (25 ml) strawberry purée

Juice of 1 mandarin orange

3 ounces (75 ml) Aperol

3 ounces (75 ml) prosecco, to finish

Strawberry slice, for garnish

Mint leaves, for garnish

Special Equipment

Muddler

Cocktail shaker

Cocktail strainer

Tall flute glass

1. In the bottom of a cocktail shaker or a big mason jar, muddle the basil leaves for 1 to 2 minutes.

2. Add ice, strawberry purée, mandarin orange juice, and Aperol. Place the lid on the shaker and shake vigorously until cold.

3. Strain into a tall flute glass. Top with the prosecco. Garnish with a thin slice of strawberry and a mint leaf.

SERVES	PREP	TOTAL
1	5 minutes	10 minutes

Spicy Watermelon Mint-Rita

This cocktail really packs a punch. It's bold, refreshing, and balances sweet and smoky flavors. Served in a chili-lime rimmed margarita glass, this cocktail is bright and zesty, perfect for a summer night.

For the rim

1 tablespoon agave nectar

Chili-lime seasoning, such as Tajín

For the cocktail

4 mint leaves

2 jalapeño slices, plus more as needed

3 ounces (75 ml) blanco tequila

Juice of 1 lime

Juice of 1 mandarin orange

4 ounces (100 ml) pure watermelon juice

Pinch of Maldon salt (a few flakes)

Sparkling water, to finish

Special Equipment

Muddler

Cocktail shaker

Cocktail strainer

1. Prepare the rim: Place the agave on a small plate and roll the rim of a margarita glass in it. Sprinkle with chili-lime seasoning. Place in the freezer to chill.

2. Make the cocktail: Add the mint and jalapeño slices to a cocktail shaker. Muddle until you have created a paste.

3. Add ice, tequila, lime juice, mandarin orange juice, and watermelon juice.

4. Place the lid on the shaker and shake vigorously until chilled.

5. Strain into the prepared glass. Top with sparkling water.

Notes

- If you want to make a frozen mint-rita, just pour all the ingredients into a blender with a handful of ice. Delicious every time!
- For a sweeter cocktail, use a lemon-lime soda in place of the sparkling water.

SERVES
1

PREP
5 minutes

TOTAL
10 minutes

Blueberry Preserves Margarita

This is such a fun way to make a cocktail! I started doing this when my fruit preserves jar was at the very end. I would just add the cocktail ingredients right into the jar, shake it up, and serve it over ice. I played around with the ratios and realized that fruit preserves are a great way to make a variety of cocktails! It allows you to add flavor and sweetness without needing to buy tons of ingredients. I prefer high-quality preserves made with real fruit, such as Bonne Maman.

2 tablespoons agave

1 teaspoon flaky salt or cane sugar

1 heaping tablespoon blueberry preserves

2 ounces (50 ml) blanco tequila

Juice of 1 lime

Juice of 1 mandarin orange

Ginger beer, to finish

Special Equipment

Cocktail shaker

Cocktail strainer

1. Place the agave on a small plate and roll the rim of your glass in it. Sprinkle with flaky salt or cane sugar, depending on your preference. Place the glass in the freezer to chill.

2. Fill a cocktail shaker with ice. Add the blueberry preserves, tequila, lime juice, and mandarin orange juice. Place the lid on the shaker and shake vigorously until cold.

3. Strain the margarita into the prepared glass. Top with the ginger beer.

Notes

- Some other jams I love to use in this cocktail are peach, strawberry, or raspberry preserves. You could also switch up the liquor here. A peach preserve and bourbon combination would be unreal!
- You can use coconut water in place of the tequila for a mocktail.

SERVES	PREP	TOTAL
1	5 minutes	10 minutes

Pomegranate and Mandarin Paloma

A colorful and vibrant twist on the classic Paloma. With the tartness of the pomegranate and the citrusy orange, this cocktail is refreshing and perfect for any day. Whether you're sipping on your couch or serving it up at your next big party, it's the perfect way to bring a little pizzazz to any occasion.

3 ounces (75 ml) tequila reposado

Juice of 1 mandarin orange

1 ounce (25 ml) pomegranate juice

Juice of 1 lime

½ ounce (12 ml) agave

Grapefruit soda, such as Fresca, to finish

Pomegranate seeds, for garnish (optional)

Grapefruit slices, for garnish (optional)

Special Equipment

Highball glass

Cocktail shaker

1. Place a highball glass in the freezer to chill.

2. Add ice, tequila, orange juice, pomegranate juice, lime juice, and agave to the shaker.

3. Place the lid on the shaker and shake vigorously until chilled.

4. Pour the cocktail into the prepared highball glass.

5. Top with grapefruit soda. Garnish with pomegranate seeds and a slice of grapefruit, if desired.

Note

- You can rim the glass with agave and flaky salt or sugar.

SERVES
1

PREP
5 minutes

TOTAL
10 minutes

Persimmon and Mandarin Cocktail

Have you ever had a persimmon? It's a bright orange fruit that is almost caramelly in flavor. It goes hand in hand with mandarins, so it's only right we created a delicious drink with the two. I recommend preparing this cocktail using the Hachiya variety of persimmons, which need to be fully soft, almost like jelly, before enjoying. With a splash of vodka and some spice from ginger, you'll have yourself a heavenly cocktail.

For the rim

2 tablespoons honey

Chili-lime seasoning, such as Tajín (optional)

Cinnamon-sugar (optional)

Flaky salt (optional)

For the cocktail

1 ripe persimmon, peeled and cut into chunks

Juice of 1 mandarin orange

Juice of 1 lemon

½ ounce (15 ml) honey (or more if you prefer it sweeter)

½ teaspoon ginger, freshly grated

2 ounces (50 ml) vodka (or bourbon, if you prefer)

½ ounce (15 ml) Cointreau

Sparkling water, to finish

Orange slice, for garnish (optional)

Cinnamon stick, for garnish (optional)

Special Equipment

Cocktail shaker

1. Prepare the rim: Drizzle the honey on a plate. Dip the rim of an old-fashioned glass in the honey, then sprinkle with your choice of rim seasoning, if desired: chili-lime seasoning, cinnamon sugar, or flaky salt. Place the glass in the freezer to chill.

2. Make the cocktail: In a cocktail shaker, add the persimmon and muddle.

3. To the shaker add ice, mandarin orange juice, lemon juice, honey, ginger, vodka, and Cointreau.

4. Place the lid on the shaker and shake vigorously until cold. Strain into the chilled old-fashioned glass.

5. Top with sparkling water. Garnish with an orange slice and cinnamon stick, if desired.

Note

- You can use ginger ale in place of the sparkling water.

SERVES
1

PREP
5 minutes

TOTAL
10 minutes

Pear Bourbon Caramel Twist

This is the most warming and comforting cocktail you will have all year! It literally tastes like pie in a glass but is still light and refreshing. The caramel and pear combo are really elite and fancy, and since fun drinks don't need alcohol, I included notes on how to make this a mocktail to cater to your lifestyle.

2 tablespoons caramel sauce

1 teaspoon flaky salt

2 ounces (50 ml) pear nectar

1 teaspoon Ceylon cinnamon

1 teaspoon honey (optional)

Juice of 1 mandarin orange

2 ounces (50 ml) bourbon

Prosecco or seltzer water, to finish

Pear slice, for garnish

Cinnamon stick, for garnish

Special Equipment

Old-fashioned glass

Cocktail shaker

Cocktail strainer

1. Spread the caramel sauce on a plate and rim one side of an old-fashioned glass, about 2 inches (5 cm) down.

2. Sprinkle the rim with flaky salt. Place the glass in the freezer to chill.

3. Fill a cocktail shaker with ice.

4. Add the pear nectar, cinnamon, honey (if using), mandarin orange juice, and bourbon. Place the lid on the shaker and shake vigorously until cold.

5. Strain the cocktail into the chilled glass. Top with prosecco or seltzer water.

6. Garnish with a thin pear slice and cinnamon stick.

Notes

- This is a great cocktail to scale up for a crowd. You can make the cocktail mix at the beginning of the day and chill before serving. Just save the bubbly for the last minute.
- To make this a mocktail, omit the bourbon, add an additional 2 ounces of pear nectar, and use seltzer in place of the prosecco.

SERVES	PREP	TOTAL
1	5 minutes	10 minutes

Cucumber Limonata Twist

Sometimes limoncello can be too sweet for me so I created this variation to tone down the sweetness and balance the flavors. Believe it or not, cucumbers are delicious in cocktails. They give the drink such a refreshing aspect and they're very hydrating.

¼ cup roughly chopped English cucumber

2 ounces (50 ml) limoncello

2 ounces (50 ml) vodka

Limonata, to finish

Lemon slice, for garnish

Cucumber, thinly sliced, for garnish

Rosemary sprig, for garnish

Special Equipment

Muddler

Cocktail shaker

Cocktail strainer

1. In the bottom of a cocktail shaker or large mason jar, muddle the cucumber.

2. Add ice, limoncello, and vodka. Place the lid on the shaker and shake vigorously until cold.

3. Strain the cocktail into a large wineglass. Top with limonata.

4. Garnish with a rosemary sprig, cucumber slice, and lemon slice.

SERVES	PREP	TOTAL
6	5 minutes (plus 8 hours freezing and 2 hours chilling time)	10 hours 5 minutes

Holiday Cheer Red Sangria

I host a lot of the holidays and Christmas is one of them. After cooking all that food, who has time to remember to prepare a cocktail? I love doing a batch cocktail for this exact reason and some variation of sangria is always a winner. This really is an elevated version of your typical sangria with a touch of seasonal spice!

1 navel orange, sliced

1 lime, sliced

1 cup cranberries

1 cup raspberries

1x (750 ml) bottle of red wine, such as cabernet sauvignon or merlot

½ cup cranberry juice

½ cup brandy (or bourbon)

½ cup apple cider

½ cup orange juice

½ cup cherry juice

2 tablespoons maple syrup

2 cinnamon sticks

¼ teaspoon freshly grated nutmeg

Seltzer water or ginger ale, to finish

Special Equipment

Parchment paper

Pitcher

1. Line a baking sheet with parchment paper. Arrange the orange slices, lime slices, cranberries, and raspberries in a single layer. Freeze for at least 8 hours.

2. In a large pitcher, add the wine, cranberry juice, brandy (or bourbon), apple cider, orange juice, cherry juice, and maple syrup. Stir.

3. Add the cinnamon sticks and grated nutmeg.

4. Chill in the fridge for at least 2 hours.

5. To serve, add some ice and a handful of frozen fruit to a wineglass. Pour in the prepared cocktail. Top with seltzer water or ginger ale.

Note

- You can use honey in place of maple syrup.

SERVES	PREP	TOTAL
1	5 minutes	10 minutes

Fizzy Lavender Lemonade

This cocktail is perfect for the ladies! It's sexy, the color is beautiful, and is a great recipe for brunch. The bright citrus really complements the floral notes of the lavender. It seems fancier than what it is. Lavender syrup is easy to find and delicious in cocktails, coffees, and baked goods!

2 ounces (50 ml) gin (or vodka if you prefer)

½ ounce (12 ml) elderflower liqueur, such as St-Germain

Juice of 2 lemons

Juice of 1 mandarin orange

1 ounce (25 ml) lavender syrup

1 ounce (25 ml) simple syrup (or honey)

Sparkling water, to finish

Lemon slice, for garnish

Special Equipment

Highball glass

Cocktail shaker

Cocktail strainer

1. Place a highball glass in the freezer to chill.

2. Fill a cocktail shaker with ice. Add the gin, elderflower liqueur, lemon juice, orange juice, lavender syrup, and simple syrup. Place the lid on the shaker and shake vigorously until cold.

3. Remove your glass from the freezer and fill with ice. Strain the cocktail into the glass. Top with sparkling water.

4. Garnish with a lemon slice.

SERVES	PREP	TOTAL
1	5 minutes	10 minutes

Chocolate Cherry Espresso Martini

Who doesn't love a cordial cherry? It's the candy you love to eat around the holidays. This is the most epic dessert cocktail—and it looks beautiful when served. If you'd prefer to make a mocktail instead, I'll walk you through how to do that.

For the rim

¼ cup freeze-dried cherries (use freeze-dried raspberries if you can't find cherries)

1 tablespoon chocolate syrup

For the cocktail

1 ounce (25 ml) vodka

1 ounce (25 ml) maraschino cherry juice

1 ounce (25 ml) brewed espresso, chilled

1 ounce (25 ml) Baileys Irish Cream

1 ounce (25 ml) coffee liqueur, such as Kahlúa

Maraschino cherries, for garnish

Dark chocolate shavings, for garnish

For the mocktail

1 ounce (25 ml) maraschino cherry juice

1 ounce (25 ml) chilled espresso

3 ounces (75 ml) macadamia milk

1 teaspoon chocolate syrup

Special Equipment

Spice grinder

Martini glass

Cocktail shaker

Cocktail strainer

1. **Prepare the rim:** Place the freeze-dried cherries in a spice grinder and grind until very fine.

2. Spread the chocolate syrup on one side of a plate and the powdered freeze-dried cherries on the other side.

3. Roll the rim of a martini glass in the chocolate, followed by the powdered cherries. Place the glass in the freezer to chill.

4. **Prepare the cocktail:** Fill a cocktail shaker with ice. Add the vodka, maraschino cherry juice, espresso, Baileys, and coffee liqueur. **For a mocktail,** add the cherry juice, espresso, macadamia milk, and chocolate syrup instead. Place the lid on the shaker and shake vigorously until cold.

5. Strain the cocktail into the prepared glass. Garnish with skewered cherries or chocolate shavings.

Baked Goods

MAKES	PREP	COOK	TOTAL
About 60 cookies	10 minutes (plus 20 minutes chilling time)	20 to 22 minutes	50 to 52 minutes

Sweet Thumbprint Cookies

These cookies are the perfect combination of buttery and sweet with a fruity filling. Easy to make and endlessly customizable with your favorite jam, they're a hit at every holiday gathering or as a simple treat to satisfy your sweet tooth. Whether you're baking with kids or just need a quick cookie fix, these will be your new go-to!

2 cups (32 tablespoons) salted butter, softened

1¼ cups granulated sugar

½ tablespoon vanilla bean paste (or pure vanilla extract)

½ teaspoon salt

4 egg yolks

4½ cups all-purpose flour

1 cup jam

Confectioners' sugar, for dusting

Special Equipment

Stand mixer

Parchment paper

Small cookie scoop (#40)

Fine-mesh sieve

1. In the bowl of a stand mixer fitted with the paddle attachment, cream together the softened butter and sugar, about 3 minutes.

2. Add the vanilla bean paste, salt, and egg yolks. Beat together until combined.

3. With the mixer running on low, slowly add in your flour, 1 cup at a time.

4. Chill the dough for 15 to 20 minutes.

5. Preheat the oven to 350°F (180°C). Line a large baking sheet with parchment paper.

6. Use a small cookie scoop (#40; 2 tablespoons) to scoop the dough. Roll the dough into small balls and place on the prepared baking sheet, leaving about 2 inches (5 cm) in between each cookie to spread. Use your fingers to lightly push down on each ball to flatten.

7. Spray the back of a wooden spoon with cooking spray. Press the spoon into the middle of the cookie to create a well. Add about 1 teaspoon fruit jam into the well of each cookie.

8. Bake for 20 to 22 minutes. Cool completely.

9. I like to dust powdered sugar on top with the fine-mesh sieve when serving, but they must be completely cool for this step. We make these during Christmastime, and during Easter. But it is the perfect everyday cookie because it's so easy to make with very minimal ingredients, and the flavor combinations are endless!

SERVES	PREP	COOK	TOTAL
8 to 10	25 minutes (plus 1 hour rising time)	55 minutes	About 2 hours 20 minutes

Sicilian Hot Pocket

Scacciata is a traditional Sicilian stuffed flatbread. Think of it like a hot pocket but with a fancier name. It is usually stuffed with some sort of vegetable and meat, like a calzone or stromboli. It's the kind of dish that feels special, but it's actually super practical. It's easy to serve and basically a one-pan meal. It even tastes great at room temperature, which makes for great leftovers.

4 tablespoons extra-virgin olive oil, divided, plus more for greasing the bowl and topping the dough

3½ cups all-purpose flour

1x ¼-ounce (7 g) packet instant yeast

1 teaspoon raw honey

1 teaspoon salt

1-pound hot Italian sausage meat, casings removed

1 small yellow onion, diced

4 garlic cloves, sliced

1 bunch Swiss chard, cleaned and shredded

1 cup ricotta

1½ cups shredded provolone

½ cup grated Pecorino Romano

2 tablespoons chopped parsley

2 tablespoons chopped oregano

Salt and freshly ground black pepper, to taste

Special Equipment

Parchment paper

Rolling pin

1. Lightly grease a large glass bowl with olive oil. Set aside.

2. In a large bowl, whisk together the flour, yeast, honey, and salt.

3. Add 1¼ cups warm water and 2 tablespoons olive oil. Stir until a shaggy dough forms.

4. Turn out onto a floured surface and knead for 8 to 10 minutes until smooth and elastic.

5. Place in the prepared bowl, cover, and let rise for 45 minutes to 1 hour until doubled in size.

6. While the dough rises, make the stuffing: Heat the remaining 2 tablespoons olive oil in a 12-inch (30 cm) skillet. Add the sausage and cook for 8 to 10 minutes until caramelized. Transfer the sausage to a plate.

7. In the same pan, add the onion and garlic and cook for about 5 minutes until softened.

8. Add the Swiss chard and cook for about 2 minutes until wilted.

9. Add the sausage back in, mix, and set it aside to cool.

10. In a separate bowl, mix the ricotta, provolone, Pecorino Romano, parsley, oregano, salt, and pepper.

11. Preheat the oven to 400°F (200°C). Line a baking sheet with parchment paper.

12. Punch down the dough and divide into two equal parts. Roll out one half into a rectangle on a lightly floured wooden surface and transfer to the baking sheet. Spread the cooled sausage-chard mixture evenly over the dough. Dollop the cheese mixture evenly over the sausage mixture and spread.

13. Roll out the remaining dough to the same size and lay over the filling. Pinch and crimp the edges with your fingers to seal completely.

14. Brush the top of the dough with olive oil. Cut a few 1-inch (2.5 cm) slits to let the steam escape.

15. Bake for 30 to 35 minutes until golden and cooked through. Let it cool for at least 10 minutes before slicing.

SERVES 8 to 10 | PREP 20 minutes | COOK 1 hour | TOTAL 1 hour 20 minutes (plus 1 hour cooling time)

Shortcut Pizza Rustica

We are using store-bought pizza dough, which makes this recipe quick and easy while still delivering that Italian flavor. You can pick it up from your local pizzeria or grocery store. This dish consists of eggs, cheese, and cured meats and is traditionally served around Easter. I like to cut it into small cubes and use that as my antipasto on holidays. We love to eat this dish at room temperature or cold from the fridge. I'm going to share my favorite flavor combination, but you can switch up the variation of meats and cheeses here.

1 cup basket cheese (or ricotta)

5 large eggs

¼ cup grated Pecorino Romano, plus more for dusting

Freshly ground black pepper, to taste

¼ cup chopped parsley

3 garlic cloves, minced

½ cup cubed hot (or sweet) soppressata

½ cup cubed mortadella

½ cup cubed Genoa salami

½ cup cubed provolone

½ cup cubed mozzarella

Extra-virgin olive oil, for greasing

2x 8-ounce (227 g) balls premade pizza dough

1 egg yolk, for the egg wash

1 tablespoon whole milk

Special Equipment

10-inch (25 cm) springform pan

Rolling pin

Pastry brush

1. Preheat the oven to 325°F (165°C).

2. In a large bowl, add in the basket cheese, eggs, Pecorino Romano, pepper, parsley, and garlic. Mix until combined.

3. Add the soppressata, mortadella, salami, provolone, and mozzarella. Mix to combine.

4. Grease a 10-inch (25 cm) springform pan with olive oil. Wrap the bottom of the pan with aluminium foil. Dust the inside with Pecorino Romano.

5. Flatten one ball of pizza dough with a rolling pin to fit the bottom and sides of an about 10-inch (25 cm) pan. Add the cheese and meat mixture.

6. Lightly flour a wooden surface. Roll out the remaining pizza dough until it is between 10 and 11 inches (25 cm and 28 cm) in diameter. Drape it over the filling. Trim the excess dough and discard.

7. In a small bowl, whisk together the egg yolk and milk. Lightly brush the top of the dough with the egg wash. Place the springform pan on a baking sheet. Bake for 50 to 60 minutes until golden brown.

8. Cool for at least one hour before releasing the pan.

MAKES	PREP	COOK	TOTAL
1 large round loaf	20 minutes (plus about 3 hours rising time)	35 minutes	4 hours

Semi-Semolina Loaf with Compound Butter

This is the easiest bread recipe you will ever make! When you make Sunday dinner, there's nothing like having fresh bread with it. I am a sourdough girl, but it can be very time consuming to make. When I want fresh bread in a few hours, this is what you will catch me whipping up. This loaf has a golden crust with a nice chewy texture. It's made with a mix of semolina and all-purpose flour. It's easy enough for even beginner bakers and requires minimal hands-on time but delivers bakery-quality results.

For the compound butter

½ cup (8 tablespoons) salted butter, softened

1 garlic clove, minced

1 teaspoon orange zest

1 tablespoon chopped basil

1 teaspoon raw honey

For the bread

Neutral oil

1x ¼-ounce (7 g) packet instant yeast

2 tablespoons raw honey

2 cups fine semolina flour

1½ cups all-purpose flour, plus more for dusting

2 teaspoons fine sea salt

2 tablespoons extra-virgin olive oil

1 teaspoon toasted sesame seeds

Flaky salt, for garnish

Special Equipment

Stand mixer

Dough hook

Large Dutch oven

1. Prepare the compound butter: In a medium bowl, mix the butter, garlic, orange zest, basil, and honey.

2. Wrap the butter in plastic wrap and store in the fridge.

3. Make the bread: Grease a large glass bowl with a neutral oil.

4. In a small bowl, mix 1¼ cups warm water, the instant yeast, and honey. Let sit for 8 to 10 minutes until frothy.

5. In the bowl of a stand mixer fitted with the dough hook, mix the semolina flour, all-purpose flour, and sea salt. Add the yeast mixture and olive oil. Mix on low with the dough hook until the dough just begins to come together.

6. Increase the speed to medium and mix for 6 to 8 minutes until the dough is smooth and elastic. Transfer the dough to the prepared bowl. Cover with a damp towel and let rise in the warmest part of your kitchen for 1½ to 2 hours until it has doubled in size. Remove the cloth and punch the dough. Lightly flour a cutting board. Transfer the dough to the board and shape it into an oval. Transfer to a large Dutch oven, cover loosely with a damp cloth, and let rise for 30 to 45 minutes.

7. Preheat the oven to 400°F (200°C).

8. Sprinkle the top of the dough with toasted sesame seeds. Bake for 30 to 35 minutes until golden brown. It should sound hollow when you tap it.

9. Remove from the pan and let it cool on a wire rack for at least 30 minutes before slicing and serving with the compound butter. Sprinkle with some flaky salt and enjoy!

MAKES	PREP	COOK	TOTAL
32 to 36 cookies	15 minutes	15 minutes	30 minutes

Seeded Cookies

Another simple cookie recipe that you should have under your belt. I can remember the smell of the sesame cookies being dipped into tea. These cookies are sometimes known as regina cookies or sesame cookies. We always called them "the cookies with the seeds." It's subtly sweet and the perfect amount of nutty from the sesame seeds.

1 cup (16 tablespoons) salted butter, softened

1 cup granulated sugar

3 whole eggs, room temperature

2 teaspoons pure almond extract

1 teaspoon salt

3 cups all-purpose flour

2 tablespoons orange zest

1 cup toasted sesame seeds

Confectioners' sugar, for dusting

Special Equipment

Electric hand mixer

Small cookie scoop (#40)

Fine-mesh sieve

1. Preheat the oven to 360°F (182°C).

2. In a large bowl, add the butter and sugar. Use an electric hand mixer or whisk to cream together for about 2 minutes.

3. Add the eggs, almond extract, and salt. Mix for 2 minutes

4. Add the flour and orange zest. Mix until it comes together.

5. Spread the sesame seeds on a plate or shallow bowl. Use a small cookie scoop (#40; 2 tablespoons) to scoop a 1.5-inch (4 cm) ball of dough and shape as desired. Dip the cookie into the sesame seeds, making sure that it's evenly coated. Place on a baking sheet. Repeat with the remaining dough.

6. Bake for 12 to 15 minutes. Cool completely.

7. Dust with confectioner's sugar.

SERVES	PREP	COOK	TOTAL
8 to 10	10 minutes	1 hour 15 minutes (plus 4 hours resting time and overnight chilling time)	12+ hours

Espresso Ricotta Cheesecake

This cheesecake is everything! Ricotta makes the texture lighter than a traditional New York-style cheesecake, while a hit of espresso wakes it all up. It's the kind of dessert that feels right after a cozy pasta dinner or dressed up for a dinner party. No water bath, no fuss—just creamy, dreamy results every time. You can get creative with the crust here; we are using ladyfingers but Biscoff cookies are amazing too.

Baking spray, for greasing

24 crispy ladyfingers

5 tablespoons salted butter, melted

½ teaspoon salt

2 pounds (907 g) whole milk ricotta, such as Galbani

¾ cup granulated sugar

2 teaspoons instant espresso powder, such as Café Bustelo

2 large eggs

3 egg yolks

¼ cup all-purpose flour

1 tablespoon vanilla bean paste

Zest of 1 lemon (about 1 tablespoon)

Confectioners' sugar, for garnish (optional)

Blueberries, for garnish (optional)

Special Equipment

9-inch (23 cm) springform pan

Food processor

Stand mixer

1. Preheat the oven to 325°F (165°C). Grease a 9-inch (23 cm) springform pan with baking spray. Wrap the bottom in aluminium foil.

2. In the bowl of a food processor fitted with the blade attachment, add the ladyfingers, melted butter, and salt. Pulse together so it looks like a dry paste. Transfer the mixture to the pan and press evenly to form a crust.

3. In the bowl of a stand mixer fitted with the paddle attachment, add the ricotta, sugar, and espresso powder. Mix for 3 minutes until fluffy.

4. Add the eggs, egg yolks, flour, vanilla bean paste, and lemon zest. Mix for about 3 minutes until combined.

5. Transfer the mixture to the springform pan. Lightly tap the pan on the counter to remove any air bubbles.

6. Bake for 1 hour and 15 minutes. Once the time has elapsed, leave the cake in the oven and do not open the door for at least 4 hours.

7. Chill in the fridge overnight.

8. Garnish with confectioner's sugar and fresh blueberries, if desired.

MAKES	PREP	COOK	TOTAL
2 braided loaves (10 to 12 servings)	15 minutes (plus 2 hours rising time)	40 minutes	3 hours

Old-School Easter Bread

This is the kind of bread you make once a year, braided with memory and meaning—aka my kids fighting over who could do which part in the recipe. It's the memories that count, am I right? This bread is soft, slightly sweet, and screams Easter. Instead of traditional dyed eggs, we will add a nice glaze and some sprinkles. It's a shame we only make it once a year, so let's change that.

For the bread

6 tablespoons salted butter, softened, plus more for greasing the bowl

1 cup warm whole milk

½ cup granulated sugar

4 large eggs, room temperature, divided

1 tablespoon vanilla bean paste

1 tablespoon orange zest

1 teaspoon salt

4¾ cups all-purpose flour, divided

1x ¼-ounce (7 g) packet instant yeast

1 tablespoon heavy cream

For the glaze

2 cups confectioners' sugar

4 to 5 tablespoons heavy cream

Nonpareils (optional)

Special Equipment

Stand mixer

Dough hook

Parchment paper

Pastry brush

1. **Prepare the bread:** Grease a large glass bowl with butter. Set aside. Line a baking sheet with parchment paper.

2. In the bowl of a stand mixer fitted with the dough hook, add the warm milk, sugar, butter, 3 eggs, vanilla bean paste, orange zest, and salt. Mix well for 2 to 3 minutes until eggs are fully broken down.

3. Gradually add in 2 cups of flour and the instant yeast. Mix for 2 minutes, then add the rest of the flour.

4. Continue to mix for 9 to 10 minutes until the dough is softer, darker in color, and springier.

5. Shape the dough into a ball and transfer to the prepared bowl. Cover with a clean, damp cloth and let it rise in the warmest part of your kitchen for 60 to 80 minutes until doubled in size.

6. Punch down the dough and divide into 6 equal pieces. Roll each piece into 12- to 14-inch (30 to 36 cm) long ropes.

7. Lay out 3 ropes on a lightly floured surface. Braid the ropes, tucking the ends underneath the loaf neatly. Place the loaf on a parchment-lined baking sheet. Repeat with the remaining ropes to create a second loaf.

8. Cover loosely and let rise for another 35 to 40 minutes or until it has puffed up again.

9. Preheat the oven to 350°F (180°C).

10. In a small bowl, whisk together the remaining egg and the cream.

11. Use a pastry brush to brush each loaf with the egg wash.

12. Bake for 35 to 40 minutes until deep golden brown. It should sound hollow when you tap it.

13. Let cool fully before glazing.

14. **Make the glaze:** In a medium mixing bowl, whisk together the confectioners' sugar and heavy cream. Dip the top of the bread in the glaze and sprinkle with the nonpareils, if desired. It's just as delicious served up plain, with a little butter on it. Such an underrated bread!

SERVES	PREP	COOK	TOTAL
8 to 10	20 minutes (plus 30 minutes resting time)	10 minutes	1 hour

Mandarin Struffoli

Now I know this is the "baked" goods section, but these are fried. Can I get a pass for this one? I promise it's worth it. They are so addicting—crunchy on the outside, pillowy on the inside, and swimming in this citrusy honey sauce. Of course, I had to put my own twist on Grammy's recipe. After all, a little mandarin zest and juice never hurt nobody!

For the struffoli

2½ cups all-purpose flour

2 tablespoons granulated sugar

1 teaspoon baking powder

1 teaspoon salt

1 tablespoon mandarin orange zest

3 large eggs, room temperature

2 tablespoons salted butter, softened

1 teaspoon vanilla bean paste

1 tablespoon mandarin orange juice

Neutral oil for frying, such as peanut or avocado oil

For the honey glaze

1¼ cup raw honey

2 tablespoons fresh mandarin orange juice

1 teaspoon mandarin orange zest

Rainbow nonpareils, for garnish (optional)

Candied citrus, for garnish (optional)

Chopped nuts, for garnish (optional)

Maraschino cherries, for garnish (optional)

Special Equipment

Stand mixer

Dough hook

Dutch oven

Candy thermometer

Slotted spoon

Wire rack

1. Prepare the struffoli: In the bowl of a stand mixer fitted with the dough hook, mix the flour, sugar, baking powder, salt, and mandarin orange zest.

2. Add the eggs, butter, vanilla bean paste, and mandarin orange juice. Mix to combine.

3. Continue to mix for 4 to 5 minutes until the dough looks smooth.

4. Cover the bowl with plastic wrap and rest at room temperature for about 30 minutes.

5. Divide the dough into six pieces and roll into 10-inch-long (25 cm) ropes. Cut the ropes into ½-inch (13 mm) pieces.

6. Heat 3 to 4 cups oil in a large, heavy-bottomed pot over medium heat until it reaches 350°F to 375°F (180°C to 190°C).

7. Working in batches to avoid overcrowding, add the dough and fry for 3 to 4 minutes, stirring occasionally. Use a slotted spoon to transfer them to a wire rack–lined baking sheet. Cool. Repeat with the remaining dough.

8. Make the honey glaze: In a small saucepan set over medium heat, add the honey, mandarin orange juice, and zest to a saucepan. Cook for about 2 minutes, stirring, until the mixture bubbles.

9. Add the fried struffoli to a large bowl. Pour the warm honey glaze over the struffoli and toss gently with a rubber spatula.

10. Transfer to a plate and create a tall pile. Immediately add toppings such as nonpareils, candied citrus, chopped nuts, or maraschino cherries, if desired.

11. Let cool for about 10 minutes before serving.

MAKES	PREP	COOK	TOTAL
30 cookies	15 minutes (plus time overnight to strain ricotta)	18 to 20 minutes	8 hours 45 minutes

Lemon Ricotta Cookies

It's no secret that I'm a huge fan of lemon. These lemon ricotta cookies are so delicate that they're basically little pillows. We owe this beautiful texture to the ricotta. They are so light and the perfect balance of tangy and sweet. The milky lemon glaze ties the whole cookie together.

For the cookies

1¼ cup whole milk ricotta

1¼ cups granulated sugar

10 tablespoons salted butter, softened

1 teaspoon vanilla bean paste or pure vanilla extract

1 large whole egg

1 large egg yolk

1 tablespoon lemon zest

3 tablespoons fresh lemon juice

1 teaspoon baking powder

1 teaspoon baking soda

½ teaspoon salt

2¼ cups all-purpose flour

For the glaze

1 cup confectioners' sugar

2 tablespoons fresh lemon juice

1 teaspoon lemon zest

1 to 2 teaspoons milk, if needed

Special Equipment

Fine-mesh sieve

Cheesecloth

Stand mixer

Parchment paper

Small cookie scoop (#50)

Wire rack

1. Prepare the cookies: Line a colander or fine-mesh sieve with cheesecloth and set it over a large bowl. Place the ricotta in the cheesecloth, cover, and chill overnight.

2. In the bowl of a stand mixer fitted with the paddle attachment, mix the sugar and butter for about 3 minutes until light and fluffy.

3. Add the vanilla, egg, egg yolk, and lemon zest. Mix for about 3 minutes until combined.

4. Add the strained ricotta, lemon juice, baking powder, baking soda, and salt. Mix for about 2 minutes until combined.

5. With the mixer running on low, gradually add the flour until the dough begins to come together. Chill, covered, in the fridge.

6. Preheat your oven to 350°F (180°C). Line two large baking sheets with parchment paper.

7. Use the small cookie scoop (#50; 1½ tablespoons) to form 1 tablespoon-size balls of dough and roll. Place them about 2 inches (5 cm) apart on the prepared baking sheet. Bake for 18 to 20 minutes. Let cool completely.

8. Prepare the glaze: Once the cookies have cooled, in a large bowl, whisk together the confectioners' sugar, lemon juice, lemon zest, and 1 teaspoon milk until smooth.

9. Dip the top of the cooled cookies into the glaze. Place on a wire rack to let the excess glaze run off. Let the cookies sit for about 10 minutes so that the glaze hardens.

MAKES	PREP	COOK	TOTAL
20 cookies	10 minutes	15 to 18 minutes	30 minutes

Gluten-Free Nutty Italian Gems

These pine nut cookies are flourless, which makes them naturally gluten-free. Whether you're looking for a classic dessert to shower your holiday table or a simple cookie to enjoy with a cup of espresso, these cookies have you covered. The crunch from the pine nuts adds texture and the almond paste provides that chewy center, making each bite a little piece of heaven. Bonus: They're quick to put together.

1 tablespoon salted butter

1½ cups pine nuts

2x 8-ounce (227 g) packages almond paste

1 cup granulated sugar

3 egg whites

¼ teaspoon salt

1 teaspoon vanilla bean paste or pure vanilla extract

Confectioners' sugar, for dusting

Special Equipment

Parchment paper

Food processor

Small cookie scoop (#40)

Wire rack

Fine-mesh sieve

1. Preheat the oven to 350°F (180°C). Line a baking sheet with parchment paper.

2. Melt the butter in a medium skillet set over medium heat. Add the pine nuts and toast for about 5 minutes, stirring frequently. Set aside.

3. In the bowl of a food processor fitted with the blade attachment, crumble the almond paste into small pieces. Add the sugar and mix for about 2 minutes.

4. Add the egg whites, salt, and vanilla bean paste. Pulse until the mixture comes together.

5. Use a small cookie scoop (#40; 2 tablespoons) to scoop the dough and roll to create a ball.

6. Roll each ball into the butter-toasted pine nuts. Do not push down—the nuts will naturally stick to the dough.

7. Place the cookies on the prepared baking sheet. Bake for 15 to 18 minutes. Cool on a wire rack. Dust with confectioners' sugar before serving.

Note

- Keep a small bowl of water nearby as you roll and shape the cookies since the dough can be sticky. Dipping your hands in the water will help make the dough more manageable.

MAKES	PREP	COOK	TOTAL
32 cookies	10 minutes (plus 30 minutes chilling time)	20 minutes	1 hour

Brown Butter Cherry Chocolate Chip Cookies

Try saying that title four times fast! This is my little twist on a classic old-school cookie. Is there a better combination than cherry and chocolate? I think not. Browning the butter here really gives these cookies a nutty flavor and the perfect chew. They are a crowd-pleaser and they look beautiful on your holiday cookie trays. All you need is a nice big glass of cold milk.

1 cup (16 tablespoons) salted butter

¾ cup granulated sugar

¾ cup light brown sugar

4 egg yolks

1 large egg

1 tablespoon vanilla bean paste or pure vanilla extract

1 teaspoon baking powder

1 teaspoon baking soda

¼ teaspoon salt

3 cups all-purpose flour

1 cup maraschino cherries, patted dry and chopped

1 cup milk chocolate chips

Special Equipment

Stand mixer

Parchment paper

1. Melt the butter in a small pan set over medium heat for about 4 minutes, just until it browns slightly and smells nutty. Set aside to cool.

2. In the bowl of a stand mixer fitted with the paddle attachment, add the cooled butter, granulated sugar, and brown sugar. Cream together for about 3 minutes.

3. Add the egg yolks, whole egg, vanilla bean paste, baking powder, baking soda, and salt. Mix for about 3 minutes until combined.

4. With the mixture running on low speed, gradually add in the flour.

5. Add the chopped cherries and chocolate chips. Mix for about 30 seconds until just combined.

6. Transfer the dough onto a sheet of parchment paper and shape it into a log (around 10 inches long, 1.5 inches thick [25 cm x 4 cm]). Chill for 30 minutes.

7. Preheat the oven to 350°F (180°C).

8. Line two large baking sheets with parchment paper.

9. Remove the log from the fridge. Slice into 1½-inch (4 cm) thick cookies.

10. Place the cookies on the prepared baking sheets, about 2 inches (5 cm) apart.

11. Bake for 18 to 20 minutes. Cool before enjoying.

MAKES	PREP	COOK	TOTAL
About 4 dozen cookies	10 minutes (plus 15 minutes chilling time)	10 to 12 minutes	40 minutes

Nonna's Everyday Cookies

I kid you not, my nonna would have these out all day, every day in a repurposed tin. Later in life when I met my husband, he shared that same memory about his grandmother, too. We laughed and said they're all the same. The truth is, times were rough back then and ingredients were scarce. They were just creating what they could with what they had. This cookie is soft and lightly sweet, perfect with coffee, and best enjoyed over some juicy family drama. These are versatile, humble, and truly made with love.

For the cookies

4 large eggs, room temperature

1 cup granulated sugar

1 cup (16 tablespoons) salted butter, softened

1 tablespoon pure vanilla extract

2 tablespoons heavy cream

4 cups all-purpose flour

1 tablespoon baking powder

1 teaspoon salt

Cooking spray

For the glaze

2 cups confectioners' sugar

4 to 5 tablespoons milk

Sprinkles, such as nonpareils (optional)

Special Equipment

Stand mixer

Parchment paper

Small cookie scoop (#40)

1. Prepare the cookies: In the bowl of a stand mixer fitted with the paddle attachment, beat the eggs for about 2 minutes until frothy.

2. With the mixer running, gradually add the sugar until the mixture has thickened.

3. Add the butter, vanilla, and heavy cream. Beat for 1 to 2 minutes until combined.

4. In a separate bowl, mix the flour, baking powder, and salt.

5. With the mixture running on low, gradually add the dry ingredients to the wet ingredients. Chill for 15 minutes in the fridge.

6. Preheat the oven to 375°F (190°C). Line two large baking sheets with parchment paper and spray them lightly with cooking spray.

7. Use a small cookie scoop (#40; 2 tablespoons) to scoop and roll the dough into balls, about 1.5 inches (4 cm). Place on a baking sheet about 2 inches (5 cm) apart.

8. Bake for 10 to 12 minutes. Cool completely.

9. Meanwhile, make the glaze: In a medium bowl, whisk together the confectioners' sugar and milk.

10. Dip the top part or half of the cookie (if you like a lot of icing) into the glaze, then sprinkle with nonpareils, if desired.

(Mostly) Meatless Meal Prep At Work

MAKES	PREP	COOK	TOTAL
4 cups	5 minutes	35 minutes	40 minutes

Basic Roasted Chickpeas

One cup of these beans contains about 15 grams of protein! This makes them one of the best meatless building blocks for any meal. They are wildly versatile and so filling.

- 3x 15-ounce (425 g) cans chickpeas
- 3 tablespoons extra-virgin olive oil
- 2 teaspoons salt
- 1 teaspoon freshly ground black pepper
- ½ teaspoon garlic powder
- ½ teaspoon onion powder
- ½ teaspoon paprika
- ½ teaspoon dried oregano
- Juice of 1 navel orange

Special Equipment

Fine-mesh sieve

1. Preheat the oven to 425°F (220°C).
2. Rinse, drain, and pat the chickpeas dry.
3. In a large bowl, add the chickpeas, oil, salt, pepper, garlic powder, onion powder, paprika, oregano, and orange juice. Toss to combine.
4. Arrange the chickpeas in a single layer on a baking sheet. Cook for 30 to 35 minutes, shaking the pan halfway through to ensure even browning. Cool completely before serving.

Storage Tips

- Store the roasted chickpeas in a paper bag at room temperature for up to 5 days. The best part is if they soften, you can crisp them up the same way you made them. Avoid putting in the fridge or freezing as it really changes consistency, so only make enough for the 5 days.

MAKES	PREP	COOK	TOTAL
3 cups	10 minutes	35 minutes	45 minutes

Basic Prepped Lentils

Do not sleep on lentils. They are budget-friendly, easy to cook, and packed with protein. They will soak up whatever flavor you cook them with. The key is to cook them until they're just tender but not mushy.

2 tablespoons extra-virgin olive oil, divided

1 carrot, cut into large chunks

1 celery stalk, cut into large chunks

1 medium shallot, halved

1 garlic clove, chopped

1 cup green or brown lentils

3 cups vegetable stock

1 dried bay leaf

Salt and freshly ground black pepper, to taste

Special Equipment

Fine-mesh sieve

1. Heat 1 tablespoon oil in a large pot set over medium heat. Add the carrots, celery, shallot, and garlic, and cook for 6 to 8 minutes.

2. Place the lentils in a fine-mesh sieve and rinse well under cold water. To the pot add the lentils, stock, bay leaf, salt, and pepper. Bring to a boil and cook, uncovered, for 20 to 25 minutes until tender.

3. Drain any excess liquid. Discard the bay leaf and vegetables. Season to taste with salt and the remaining olive oil while warm to prevent sticking. Toss gently to combine.

Note

- Serve with arugula and lemon juice for a quick salad or swirl into soups and stews for a boost of protein.

Storage Tips

- Let the lentils cool before storing. They will last in the fridge for up to 5 days or up to 3 months in the freezer.

SERVES	PREP	COOK	TOTAL
6	10 minutes (plus 30 minutes pressing time and 10 minutes to marinate)	40 minutes	1 hour 30 minutes

Basic Baked Tofu

Tofu is one of those things that people think they hate until they've actually had it prepped right. It's simple and crispy around the edges and full of umami flavor. It holds up so well in the fridge, and is so adaptable to whatever seasonings or sauces you're in the mood for that day.

2x 16-ounce (454 g) blocks extra-firm tofu, drained

2 tablespoons soy sauce

2 tablespoons avocado oil

2 garlic cloves, grated

1 tablespoon rice vinegar

1 tablespoon maple syrup

Salt and freshly ground black pepper, to taste

Special Equipment

Cast-iron skillet

Parchment paper

Slotted spoon

1. To remove the excess moisture from the tofu, wrap the blocks of tofu in paper towels and place them on a plate. Place a heavy pot or cast-iron skillet on top of them. Allow the tofu to drain for 30 minutes.

2. Preheat the oven to 425°F (220°C). Line a medium-size baking sheet with parchment paper.

3. Cut the tofu into cubes or slices. In a large bowl, whisk together the soy sauce, oil, garlic, rice vinegar, maple syrup, salt, and pepper.

4. Add the tofu and let it marinate while your oven preheats, about 10 minutes.

5. Use a slotted spoon to remove the tofu cubes from the marinade and place on the prepared baking sheet. Bake for 35 to 40 minutes, flipping halfway through, until golden and slightly crispy.

Storage Tips

- This will last in your fridge for up to 5 days and it's super freezer friendly. It will last there up to 2 months, and you could reheat it straight from the freezer. Either 8 minutes in the air fryer or pan frying back up to temperature will do the trick.

SERVES	PREP	COOK	TOTAL
4	5 minutes	15 minutes	20 minutes

Stir-Fried Veggies and Tofu

I like to think of this as a "kitchen sink stir-fry" because it's the perfect place to use up whatever roasted or raw veggies you have on hand. I love to serve this over rice, noodles, or even in lettuce cups.

2 tablespoons avocado oil

1 small yellow onion, sliced (about ¼ cup)

4 garlic cloves, grated

1 teaspoon grated fresh ginger

3 cups chopped mixed vegetables, such as broccoli, peppers, cabbage, and mushrooms

2 cups cubed Basic Baked Tofu (see page 178)

3 tablespoons soy sauce

3 tablespoons hoisin sauce

Juice of 2 limes (about ¼ cup)

Chopped scallions, for garnish

Chopped cilantro, for garnish

Chili oil, for garnish

Sticky rice, for serving

1. Heat the oil in a large skillet set over medium heat.

2. Add the onion and cook for 2 to 3 minutes.

3. Add the garlic and ginger and cook for about 2 minutes until fragrant.

4. Add the vegetables to the pan. Cook for 1 to 2 minutes for precooked, 4 to 5 minutes for raw vegetables.

5. Stir in the cubed baked tofu and let it heat through, 2 to 3 minutes.

6. In a small bowl, whisk together the soy sauce, hoisin sauce, and lime juice. Add to the tofu-veggie mixture. Cook for about 5 minutes.

7. Serve on a bed of sticky rice and top with scallions, cilantro, and chili oil.

SERVES 4 | **PREP** 10 minutes | **TOTAL** 10 minutes

Chickpea Pitas

We all have those days when we're hungry, short on time, and looking at our fridge like it's going to do the cooking. That's when I reach for my batch of preroasted chickpeas, add some vegetables and seasonings, and stuff some pita pockets. They're crunchy, fresh, and loaded with flavor. Plus, you can stuff them with whatever veggies you've got leftover from the night before.

2 cups Basic Roasted Chickpeas (see page 176)

½ cup coleslaw mix

1 cup diced cucumbers

½ cup halved cherry tomatoes

¼ cup thinly sliced red onion

1 tablespoon extra-virgin olive oil

Juice of 1 lemon

1 teaspoon red wine vinegar

2 tablespoons chopped oregano

½ cup crumbled feta

Salt and freshley ground black pepper, to taste

4 pita pockets

½ cup plain Greek yogurt

Special Equipment

Toaster

1. In a large bowl, add the roasted chickpeas, coleslaw mix, cucumbers, cherry tomatoes, red onions, olive oil, lemon juice, red wine vinegar, oregano, and feta. Season to taste with salt and pepper. Stir. Set aside and allow it to marinate.

2. Warm the pitas, uncut, in the toaster, 2 to 3 minutes.

3. Slice the pitas and spread the Greek yogurt on the inside on both sides.

4. Evenly divide the chickpea mixture between each pita. Serve immediately.

Note

- You can substitute 1 teaspoon of dried oregano for the fresh oregano.

SERVES 4 | **PREP** 10 minutes | **TOTAL** 10 minutes

Tuna and Chickpea Salad

Protein-packed and pantry-friendly, this is a meal that is fast and flavorful. The chickpeas bring a nice crunch and creaminess. This works for lunch or dinner, on a wrap, on a roll, or on a bed of lettuce.

2x 5-ounce (142 g) cans of tuna packed in oil, drained

1 cup Basic Roasted Chickpeas (see page 176)

1 celery stalk, finely chopped

1 scallion, finely chopped

1 English cucumber, diced

1 tablespoon capers

2 tablespoons sliced almonds

4 tablespoons mayonnaise

1 tablespoon Dijon mustard

Juice of 1 lemon

¼ cup finely chopped roasted red peppers

Salt and freshly ground black pepper, to taste

Salad greens, for serving

Pita pockets, tortillas, or bread slices, for serving (optional)

1. In a large bowl, add the tuna, roasted chickpeas, celery, scallions, cucumber, capers, sliced almonds, mayonnaise, mustard, lemon juice, and roasted peppers. Season to taste with salt and pepper. Stir.

2. To serve, spoon over greens for a salad or packed into pita, wraps, or sandwiches.

SERVES	PREP	COOK	TOTAL
4	5 minutes	20 minutes	25 minutes

Roasted Tofu and Veggie Tacos

This is sheet pan cooking at its finest! We just toss everything with some dried spices, roast it up, and pile high on tortillas. The baked tofu gets slightly crispy in the oven, the veggies caramelize beautifully, and it all comes together with a squeeze of lime and some help from the condiment shelf in your fridge.

- 2 cups cubed Basic Baked Tofu (see page 178)
- 1 small bell pepper, diced
- 1 small red onion, diced
- 1 medium zucchini, diced
- 2 tablespoons extra-virgin olive oil
- 1 teaspoon chili powder
- 1 teaspoon ground cumin
- 1 teaspoon turmeric
- 1 tablespoon honey
- Juice of 1 lime
- Salt and freshly ground black pepper, to taste
- 8 medium-size flour tortillas

For serving (optional)

- Queso fresco or cotija
- Avocado slices
- Chopped cilantro
- Sour cream
- Salsa
- Shredded lettuce
- Pickled jalapeños

1. Preheat the oven to 425°F (220°C).

2. Arrange the baked tofu, bell pepper, red onion, zucchini, olive oil, chili powder, cumin, turmeric, honey, lime juice, salt, and pepper on a large baking sheet. Toss to combine.

3. Bake for 18 to 20 minutes.

4. Meanwhile, warm the tortillas in a dry pan or microwave wrapped in a damp paper towel for 30 to 40 seconds.

5. To serve, divide the mixture evenly between the tortillas. Garnish with the desired toppings.

MAKES	PREP	COOK	TOTAL
1 Mezze plate	10 minutes	10 minutes	20 minutes

Baked Tofu Mezze Plate

Mezze plate is really just a fancy word for saying, "I am definitely NOT cooking tonight." It's the perfect solution for weeknights when you want something low effort but high reward with a mix of color, texture, and flavor. Think of it like a Mediterranean-inspired antipasto but balanced enough to call it "dinner." Add whatever roasted or raw veggies you have on hand and let everyone build their own perfect bite. It's fun, customizable, and a great break for this busy mom.

- 1 tablespoon extra-virgin olive oil, plus more for garnish
- 1 block Basic Baked Tofu, sliced (see page 178)
- 2 garlic naan bread
- 1 cup Basic Roasted Chickpeas (see page 176)
- ¼ cup hummus
- ¼ cup tzatziki
- ¼ cup whole cherry tomatoes
- ¼ cup Kalamata olives
- ¼ cup halloumi cheese
- ¼ cup sliced bell pepper
- Handful of fresh herbs (parsley and dill recommended)
- 4 dolmas
- 4 artichoke hearts, canned
- Lemon wedges, for garnish (optional)
- Flaky salt, for garnish (optional)

1. Heat 1 tablespoon oil in a medium skillet set over medium heat. Add the tofu and cook 3 to 5 minutes per side until crispy.

2. Warm the naan in a dry pan or in the toaster for 2 to 3 minutes until warm and crispy.

3. On a large cutting board or serving platter, transfer the roasted chickpeas, hummus, and tzatziki to small bowls. Evenly arrange the cherry tomatoes, Kalamata olives, halloumi, bell peppers, herbs, dolmas, artichoke hearts, and lemon wedges on the platter. Season to taste with flaky salt. Serve immediately.

SERVES	PREP	COOK	TOTAL
5	15 minutes	50 minutes	1 hour 5 minutes

Shroomy Lentil Shepherd's Pie

This is one of my favorite ways to stretch leftovers into something totally new. If you've got mashed potatoes in the fridge and a batch of cooked lentils, you're halfway to dinner. The lentils and mushrooms create a rich, savory filling that hits all the "meaty" notes without any actual meat.

- Cooking spray
- 2 tablespoons extra-virgin olive oil
- 1 small white onion, diced
- 1 carrot, peeled and diced
- 1 celery stalk, diced
- 2 garlic cloves, chopped
- 2 cups chopped mixed mushrooms
- 1 tablespoon tomato paste
- 2 tablespoons Gravy Master
- ½ cup red wine (or vegetable stock)
- 2 cups Basic Prepped Lentils (see page 177)
- 3 cups leftover mashed potatoes
- ½ cup shredded Gruyère
- Sliced scallions, for garnish (optional)

Special Equipment

9-inch (23 cm) square baking dish

1. Preheat the oven to 400°F (200°C).

2. Lightly grease a 9-inch (23 cm) square baking dish with cooking spray.

3. Heat the oil in a large skillet set over medium heat. Add the onion, carrot, celery, garlic, and mushrooms. Cook for about 10 minutes until softened.

4. Add the tomato paste and cook for about 6 minutes until the mixture darkens in color.

5. Add the Gravy Master and red wine (or stock). Cook for about 5 minutes.

6. Add the cooked lentils. Stir and set aside.

7. In a separate bowl, combine the leftover mashed potatoes and Gruyère.

8. Transfer the lentil mixture into the prepared baking dish. Top with the mashed potatoes and spread in an even layer.

9. Bake for 25 to 30 minutes until the top is crispy.

10. Cool for 5 minutes before serving. Top with scallions, if desired.

MAKES	PREP	COOK	TOTAL
16 meatballs	15 minutes	35 minutes	50 minutes to 1 hour

Roasted Lentil and Eggplant "Meatballs"

This is the kind of meatless comfort food that makes you forget all about the meat. The eggplant gives these meatballs a silky texture and earthy depth, while the lentils add that hearty bite and a protein boost.

2 tablespoons extra-virgin olive oil, divided

1 small white onion, finely diced

1 small bell pepper, finely diced

4 garlic cloves, grated

Salt and freshly ground black pepper, to taste

1 whole roasted eggplant, skin discarded

1½ cups Basic Prepped Lentils (see page 177)

½ cup Italian-seasoned breadcrumbs, plus more as needed

½ cup grated Pecorino Romano

1 large egg

2 tablespoons chopped parsley

Special Equipment

Cookie scoop (#50)

Parchment paper

1. Preheat the oven to 400°F (200°C)

2. Heat 1 tablespoon oil in a large skillet set over medium heat. Add the onions, peppers, garlic, salt, and pepper. Cook for about 10 minutes until caramelized. Set aside.

3. Line a large baking sheet with parchment paper and lightly oil it with the remaining tablespoon of olive oil.

4. In a large bowl, combine the roasted eggplant and cooked lentils. Mash together with a fork or potato masher until cohesive.

5. Add the breadcrumbs, Pecorino Romano, egg, sautéed vegetables, parsley, salt, and pepper. If the mixture is too soft to roll, add breadcrumbs, 1 tablespoon at a time, until you reach your desired consistency.

6. Use a cookie scoop (#50; 1½ tablespoons) to form about 1½ tablespoons of the mixture and roll into balls. Place on the prepared baking sheet, spacing them slightly apart.

7. Bake for 20 to 25 minutes, flipping halfway through, until golden and slightly firm to the touch.

Note

- I like to serve these meatballs with pasta marinara or piled high on a slice of crusty Semi-Semolina Loaf (see page 158) with melted cheese. If you want to go a different route, serve with hummus or tzatziki

MAKES	PREP	COOK	TOTAL
4 burgers	10 minutes (plus 10 to 15 minutes chilling time)	30 minutes	55 minutes

Good ol' American Lentil Cheese "Burgers"

Think of this as your go-to veggie burger when you're craving that classic diner-style cheeseburger. Instead of meat, we're using precooked lentils, which are seasoned with a bunch of burger-inspired spices. Pile the patties on a soft potato bun with all the fixings and it will taste like the Fourth of July!

1½ cups Basic Prepped Lentils (see page 177)

1 teaspoon onion powder

1 teaspoon garlic powder

1 teaspoon smoked paprika

1 teaspoon Lawry's seasoned salt

1 tablespoon tomato paste

1 teaspoon yellow mustard

1 tablespoon Worcestershire sauce

½ cup Italian-seasoned breadcrumbs, plus more as needed

1 large egg

Salt and freshly ground black pepper, to taste

2 tablespoons avocado oil

4 slices American cheese

4 potato buns

For serving (optional)

Lettuce

Sliced tomatoes

Sliced pickles

Sliced onions

1. In a large bowl, add the lentils, onion powder, garlic powder, paprika, and Lawry's seasoned salt. Mix to combine, mashing the cooked lentils with a fork.

2. Add the tomato paste, mustard, Worcestershire, breadcrumbs, and egg. Mix to combine. Season with salt and pepper.

3. Divide the mixture into 4 equal portions and shape into burger patties. If the mixture is too wet, add breadcrumbs, 1 tablespoon at a time, until you reach your desired texture.

4. Chill the patties in the fridge for 10 to 15 minutes.

5. Heat the oil in a large nonstick skillet.

6. Cook the patties for 6 to 8 minutes per side until golden and crispy. In the last minute of cooking, top each patty with a slice of American cheese. Cover to melt the cheese.

7. Toast the buns and serve with desired toppings.

Note

- You may use lettuce wraps in place of burger buns.

Storage Tip

- These freeze so well, just wrap individually in plastic wrap and freeze for up to 3 months.

Chicken Meal Prep At Work

SERVES	PREP	COOK	TOTAL
6	10 minutes	18 minutes	30 minutes

Basic Versatile Ground Chicken (or Turkey!)

Ground chicken doesn't get the same love as beef or pork, but it should. It's quick, budget-friendly, and takes on seasoning like a champ. This version is super simple with just enough flavor to stand on its own but flexible enough to incorporate into whatever you're vibing with that day.

3 tablespoons extra-virgin olive oil

1 medium shallot, minced

2 garlic cloves, grated

2 pounds (907 g) ground chicken

1 tablespoon Maggi seasoning sauce (or Worcestershire sauce)

½ teaspoon ground paprika

Salt and freshly ground black pepper

1. In a large frying pan set over medium heat, add the olive oil. Once shimmering, add the shallot and cook for 3 to 4 minutes until soft and translucent.

2. Add the garlic, stir, and cook for 1 to 2 minutes. Add the ground chicken, Maggi seasoning sauce, paprika, salt, and pepper. Use a wooden spoon or spatula to break up the meat and cook, stirring occasionally, for 10 to 12 minutes, until fully cooked and no longer pink.

Storage Tips

- Store the cooked chicken in an airtight container for up to 4 days in the fridge or divide into zip-top bags and freeze for up to 2 months.

MAKES	PREP	COOK	TOTAL
About 4 cups	10 minutes	30 minutes	40 minutes (4 hours for the slow cooker)

Basic Savory Shredded Chicken

This isn't bland boiled chicken that tastes like regret. This is seasoned, juicy, pull-apart, and endlessly useful chicken. I like to make this in my Dutch oven but it's also great in a slow cooker. I included the method for both.

2 tablespoons unsalted butter

2 garlic cloves, chopped

1 small white onion, chopped

2 pounds (907 g) boneless, skinless chicken breast

Salt and freshly ground black pepper

2 cups chicken stock

1 tablespoon apple cider vinegar

2 tablespoons chicken bouillon powder

1 bay leaf

Special Equipment

Slow cooker (optional)

1. Method for stovetop: Heat butter in the bottom of a large, deep pot over medium heat. Add the garlic and onion and slightly fry for 3 to 5 minutes.

2. Season the chicken breast with salt and pepper and sear in the butter with the onions and garlic, about 4 minutes each side.

3. Pour in the stock and apple cider vinegar, then stir in the chicken bouillon, bay leaf, and more black pepper. Bring to a gentle boil, then immediately lower the heat to a simmer. Cover and cook for 20 minutes (depending on thickness), or until the chicken is fully cooked (165°F/74°C) and shreds easily with two forks.

4. Remove the chicken and let cool slightly. Shred with two forks (or a hand mixer if you feel like washing it, but who ever does?). Add a little of the cooking liquid back in to keep it juicy, if needed.

5. Method For slow cooker: Add all the ingredients to the slow cooker.

6. Cover and cook on low for 4 hours.

7. Shred the chicken and return it to the slow cooker for 10 to 15 minutes to soak in some of the juices before serving or storing.

Storage Tips

- Store in a container with a splash of the cooking liquid for up to 4 days. Or you could freeze in portion-sized bags with some of the liquid for up to 2 months. Make sure to thaw in the fridge overnight.

Bonus Tip

- DO NOT THROW OUT THAT FLAVORFUL BROTH YOU JUST CREATED! Here is a list of uses for that liquid gold:
    - Base for a chicken soup
    - Base to cook lentils, beans, or split peas
    - Base to cook grains like rice and quinoa
    - Starter for a pan sauce or gravy
    - Save to mix into the leftovers or even freeze for later use

SERVES	PREP	COOK	TOTAL
6	10 minutes (plus 30 minutes to 2 hours to marinate)	20 minutes	1 to 3 hours

Indoor Grilled Chicken

Consider this the not-so-boring building block for easy and delicious meals all week. This reliable, versatile staple will make any week taste better, guaranteed.

- 2 pounds (907 g) boneless, skinless chicken breast
- 2 garlic cloves, grated
- 3 tablespoons extra-virgin olive oil
- 1 tablespoon honey
- Juice of 1 lemon (about 2 tablespoons)
- Juice of 1 orange (about 3 tablespoons)
- 2 teaspoons Lawry's seasoned salt or Cavender's Greek seasoning
- Freshly ground black pepper, to taste
- 1 tablespoon avocado oil

Special Equipment

Parchment paper

Meat mallet

Grill pan

Zip-top bag

Meat thermometer

1. Place the chicken breast between two pieces of parchment paper or plastic wrap. Use a meat mallet to lightly pound until about ½-inch (13 mm) thick.

2. In a large bowl, whisk together the garlic, olive oil, honey, lemon juice, orange juice, Lawry's seasoned salt, and pepper.

3. In a large zip-top bag, add the chicken and the marinade. Chill in the fridge to marinate for at least 30 minutes or up to 2 hours.

4. Heat a large grill pan over medium-high heat.

5. Add the avocado oil to the pan.

6. Grill the chicken for 5 to 7 minutes per side until evenly browned. Don't crowd the pan—cook in batches if needed. Look for nice browning and don't move it around too much. Also, if the chicken sticks to the pan, it's just not ready to be flipped yet. Give it another minute or 2 and it will release from the pan.

7. If you are unsure if your chicken is cooked, never be afraid to use your meat thermometer. Numbers don't lie and you want the internal temperature to be 165°F (73.9°C). Make sure to rest before slicing, about 5 minutes.

Storage Tips

- Store in the fridge for up to 4 days or freeze in a zip-top bag for up to 2 months. Defrost in the fridge overnight.

MAKES	PREP	COOK	TOTAL
16 cutlets	20 minutes	10 minutes	30 minutes

Basic Fried Chicken Cutlets

If there's one recipe every Italian-American family has a version of, it's chicken cutlets. Mine are thin, crispy, and seasoned to perfection. I like to batch these and keep extras in the fridge or freezer. They reheat so well in the oven or air fryer.

4 boneless skinless chicken breasts, about 5 ounces (140 g) each

4 large eggs

1 tablespoon whole milk

1 teaspoon onion powder, divided

1 teaspoon garlic powder, divided

Salt and freshly ground black pepper, to taste

3 cups Italian-seasoned breadcrumbs

¾ cup grated Pecorino Romano

2 tablespoons chopped parsley (or 1 tablespoon of dried parsley)

½ cup avocado oil, plus more as needed

Special Equipment

Zip-top bag

Meat mallet

Parchment paper

1. Slice each chicken breast into four even pieces. Place each piece between two layers of plastic wrap, parchment paper, or in a large zip-top bag and gently pound to about ¼-inch (6 mm) thick. Set aside.

2. In a large bowl, whisk together the eggs, milk, ½ teaspoon onion powder, ½ teaspoon garlic powder, salt, and pepper.

3. In a separate large bowl, combine the breadcrumbs, Pecorino Romano, remaining onion powder and garlic powder, the parsley, salt, and pepper.

4. In a large skillet, add the avocado oil.

5. Dip one chicken cutlet into the egg wash, followed by the breadcrumb mixture, making sure that the crumbs adhere to the cutlet. Transfer to a plate to rest while the oil heats up and repeat with the remaining cutlets (see Note).

6. Add your cutlets to the skillet and fry 3 to 4 minutes per side until they are golden brown.

Note

- There are two ways to tell if your oil is hot: Either sprinkle some breadcrumbs right into the oil or dip a wooden spoon in the oil and see if bubbles form.

Storage Tips

- Store leftovers in a container for up to 3 to 4 days. To freeze, cool completely, layer between parchment paper, and freeze. To reheat, place in a 375°F (190°C) oven or air fryer for 7 to 10 minutes until crispy.

SERVES
4

PREP
5 min

TOTAL
15 minutes

Weeknight Grilled Chicken Salad

Get a load of this creamy, crunchy, sweet, and savory chicken salad! It's perfect for a weeknight or delicious enough for a brunch. Serve this piled high on toasted sourdough, multigrain bread, or even a croissant.

3 cutlets of Indoor Grilled Chicken (see page 194), cut into bite-size pieces

12 green grapes, quartered

1 celery stalk, thinly sliced

¼ cup chopped walnuts

¼ cup fresh dill (or any fresh herbs you have on hand)

½ cup broccoli slaw

2 tablespoons poppy seed dressing

2 tablespoons sour cream

½ cup mayonnaise

1 teaspoon Dijon mustard

Juice of 1 lemon (about 2 tablespoons)

Salt and freshly ground black pepper, to taste

1. In a large bowl, add the chicken, grapes, celery, walnuts, dill, broccoli slaw, poppy seed dressing, sour cream, mayonnaise, mustard, lemon juice, salt, and pepper. Toss to combine.

SERVES	PREP	COOK	TOTAL
4	5 minutes	15 minutes	20 minutes

Creamy Pesto Chicken and Gnocchi

A 15-minute meal that feels like a hug in a bowl, even though it started with leftovers. You've got grilled chicken and a pack of gnocchi? Toss it all in a creamy pesto sauce loaded with fresh garlic and cheese for one delicious dinner. You can add spinach, peas, or whatever's hanging around in your fridge that's screaming to be used.

1x 16-ounce (454 g) package shelf-stable or refrigerated gnocchi

½ cup prepared pesto

2 garlic cloves, minced

1 cup heavy cream

½ cup grated Pecorino Romano, plus more for garnish

2 cups sliced Indoor Grilled Chicken (see page 194)

Salt and freshly ground black pepper, to taste

1 cup baby spinach

Crushed red pepper flakes, for garnish

1. Bring a large pot of salted water to a boil over high heat. Cook the gnocchi according to package directions. Drain.

2. In a large skillet set over medium heat, add the pesto and garlic. Cook for about 1 minute until fragrant.

3. Stir in the cream and bring to a gentle simmer, 4 to 5 minutes.

4. Reduce the heat and stir in the Pecorino Romano. Cook for 3 to 5 minutes, until the cheese has melted and the sauce has thickened, stirring frequently.

5. Stir in the cooked chicken and gnocchi. Toss to coat. Cook for 1 to 2 minutes. Season with salt and black pepper.

6. Stir in the baby spinach and cook until just wilted. Garnish with crushed red pepper flakes and Pecorino Romano. Serve immediately.

SERVES
4

PREP
15 minutes

TOTAL
15 minutes

Fridge Cleanout Chopped Salad

This is not your average side salad—this is the main event. Loaded with grilled chicken, salty salami, and creamy provolone, this chopped salad hits every craving. It's perfect for meal prep, family dinner, or that "I should eat something green" moment. Make sure to chop everything to the same size so you can get the perfect bite every time.

2 cups Indoor Grilled Chicken (see page 194), chopped into bite-size pieces

½ cup chopped salami

½ cup chopped provolone

1x 15.5-ounce (439 g) can chickpeas, rinsed and drained

2 cups chopped romaine lettuce

½ cup quartered cherry tomatoes

¼ cup diced red onion

¼ cup chopped pepperoncini

¼ cup chopped black olives

1 English cucumber, chopped (least ½ cup)

¼ cup extra-virgin olive oil

¼ cup red wine vinegar

1 teaspoon Dijon mustard

3 garlic cloves, finely minced

1 teaspoon honey

Salt and freshly ground black pepper, to taste

1. In a large bowl, add the chicken, salami, provolone, chickpeas, lettuce, cherry tomatoes, onion, pepperoncini, black olives, and cucumber. Set aside.

2. In a small mason jar, add the olive oil, vinegar, mustard, garlic, honey, salt, and pepper. Seal with the lid and shake vigorously until emulsified. Season to taste.

3. Pour the vinaigrette over the salad and toss.

4. Serve immediately.

SERVES
4

PREP
10 minutes

COOK
30 minutes

TOTAL
40 minutes

Chicken and Artichoke Pizza

We're keeping things simple with a store-bought crust and precooked chicken. A homemade white sauce brings it back to life. It's indulgent, satisfying, and ridiculously easy to pull off on a weeknight. Canned artichokes are so underrated—and this recipe proves that.

2 tablespoons salted butter

1 small shallot or onion, minced (about ¼ cup)

3 garlic cloves, minced

2 tablespoons all-purpose flour

1 cup whole milk

½ cup grated Pecorino Romano, plus more for garnish

Salt and freshly ground black pepper, to taste

1 tablespoon chopped parsley

1 store-bought pizza crust (about 1 pound/227 g)

1 tablespoon extra-virgin olive oil

1x 14-ounce (397 g) can artichoke hearts in water, drained and dried, quartered

1 cup cooked chicken, chopped (see Notes)

½ cup shredded mozzarella

½ cup shredded provolone

Crushed red pepper flakes, for garnish

1. Preheat the oven to 500°F (260°C).

2. Melt the butter in a small saucepan set over medium heat. Add the shallot or onion and cook for 5 to 8 minutes until caramelized.

3. Add the garlic and cook for 1 minute until fragrant.

4. Add the flour and cook for 1 minute, whisking constantly. Slowly add the milk and cook for 5 minutes, whisking constantly, until thickened.

5. Stir in the Pecorino Romano, salt, pepper, and parsley. Remove from heat.

6. Place the pizza crust on a baking sheet or pizza stone. Drizzle both sides of the crust with the oil. Bake for 5 minutes.

7. Remove from the oven and flip.

8. Spread the white sauce evenly over the crust. Top with the artichokes, chicken, mozzarella, and provolone. Bake for 8 to 10 minutes, rotating the pan halfway through. The cheese should be bubbly, and the crust will be nice and golden.

9. Cool for 5 minutes before slicing and serving. Garnish with crushed red pepper flakes and grated Pecorino Romano.

Notes

- You can use 1 teaspoon of dried Italian seasoning in place of the parsley.
- You can use Indoor Grilled Chicken (see page 194) or Basic Fried Chicken Cutlets (see page 195) for the chicken.

SERVES	PREP	COOK	TOTAL
2	5 minutes	10 to 12 minutes	15 to 20 minutes

Salty and Sweet Chicken Flatbreads

This flatbread will blow your mind! And remember you can use what you have on hand! You can use a lavash or even pita bread. This is a salty-and-sweet-lover's dream: salt from the goat cheese, sweet from the peaches. Perfect for a light dinner or even brunch with a little bubbly.

2 naan flatbreads (or any flatbread you like)

1 tablespoon extra-virgin olive oil

¾ cup shredded Fontina

2 garlic cloves, minced

1 cup cooked chicken, shredded (see Note)

1 large ripe peach, thinly sliced

½ cup crumbled goat cheese

1 tablespoon chopped thyme

½ cup arugula

Hot honey, for serving

1. Preheat the oven to 425°F (220°C). Line a baking sheet with parchment paper.
2. Place the naan on the prepared baking sheet. Brush both sides with the olive oil.
3. Divide the shredded Fontina and minced garlic between both pieces of naan.
4. Divide the shredded chicken and peach slices between the naan. Top with crumbled goat cheese and chopped thyme.
5. Bake for 10 for 12 minutes, or until the cheese is melted and bubbly, and the edges are golden.
6. Remove from the oven. Evenly distribute the arugula while hot so it wilts a little bit.
7. Drizzle with hot honey, slice into wedges, and serve warm.

Note

- You can use Basic Savory Shredded Chicken (see page 193) for the chicken.

SERVES	PREP	COOK	TOTAL
4	10 minutes	25 minutes	35 minutes

Shredded Chicken and Bean Stew

This meal is the perfect weeknight option because it's hearty, nutritious, and so comforting! Everyone can use something a little comforting on the weekdays.

- 2 tablespoons extra-virgin olive oil
- 1 small yellow onion, diced
- 2 celery stalks, sliced
- 1 carrot, diced small
- 4 garlic cloves, minced
- 2 tablespoons chopped fresh herbs (thyme, rosemary, and tarragon are great)
- 1x 14.5-ounce (411 g) can diced fire-roasted tomatoes
- 6 cups chicken stock
- 2 tablespoons chicken bouillon powder
- 1x 15-ounce (425 g) can cannellini beans, not drained
- 2 cups cooked chicken, shredded (see Note)
- ¾ cup small pasta, such as ditalini
- 3 cups escarole
- Salt and freshly ground black pepper, to taste
- Grated Pecorino Romano, for serving
- Semi-Semolina Loaf (see page 158) (optional, but HIGHLY encouraged)
- Lemon wedges, for serving

1. Heat the olive oil in a large pot set over medium heat. Add the onion, celery, and carrots. Cook for 3 to 5 minutes until softened.

2. Stir in the garlic and herbs. Cook for 1 minute, until fragrant.

3. Pour in the fire-roasted tomatoes, chicken stock, and chicken bouillon. Stir to combine and bring to a boil.

4. Once boiling, add the cannellini beans in liquid, shredded chicken, and pasta. Reduce the heat to low and cook for 10 to 12 minutes, until the pasta is tender.

5. Stir in the escarole and let it wilt for 2 to 3 minutes. Season to taste with salt and pepper.

6. Transfer to a large bowl and top with Pecorino Romano. Serve with some Semi-Semolina Loaf (see page 158) and lemon wedges.

Note

- You can use Basic Savory Shredded Chicken (see page 193) for the chicken.

SERVES
4

PREP
5 minutes

TOTAL
10 minutes

The Ultimate Chicken Cutlet Sandwich

How about the ultimate chicken cutlet sandwich? I'm going to walk you through one of my favorite combos, but if you have delicious, pickled items in your fridge or some marinated vegetables, this is a great place to use them. I like to make one big sandwich for the whole table and serve it family-style.

1 loaf Italian bread

4 to 5 chicken cutlets (leftovers work great!) (see Note)

6 slices of fresh mozzarella

6 sun-dried tomatoes

1 roasted red pepper, cut into strips

½ cup fresh arugula

Extra-virgin olive oil, for serving

Balsamic glaze, for serving

1. Slice the Italian loaf in half horizontally. Scoop out some of the inside to make room for the fillings.

2. In an even layer, layer the chicken cutlets, mozzarella, sun-dried tomatoes, roasted red peppers, and fresh arugula.

3. Drizzle with olive oil and balsamic glaze.

4. Place the top half of the bread on and press gently. Slice into 4 portions.

Note

- You can use Indoor Grilled Chicken (see page 194) for the chicken.

SERVES	PREP	COOK	TOTAL
5	15 minutes	10 minutes	25 minutes

Herb and Feta Bowtie Salad with Grilled Chicken

This Mediterranean-inspired bowtie salad is a 20-minute meal that feels fresh, balanced, and super satisfying. It's the perfect combo of bright herbs and salty feta, which makes it feel special, even when it's made from leftovers.

- 1 pound (454 g) farfalle
- ½ cup extra-virgin olive oil
- ½ cup red wine vinegar
- 1 teaspoon Dijon mustard
- 2 tablespoons honey
- 1 teaspoon dried oregano
- Salt and freshly ground black pepper, to taste
- 3 grilled chicken breasts, diced (see Note)
- 1 cup quartered cherry tomatoes
- ½ cup diced cucumbers
- ½ cup thinly sliced red onion
- Kalamata olives, halved
- 1 cup crumbled feta
- 3 garlic cloves, minced
- ¼ cup chopped parsley
- ¼ cup chopped dill

1. Bring a large pot of salted water to a boil. Cook the farfalle according to package directions, drain.

2. Meanwhile, make the dressing: In a mason jar, add the olive oil, vinegar, mustard, honey, oregano, salt, and pepper. Seal with the lid and shake vigorously until combined.

3. In a large bowl, combine the farfalle, chicken, tomatoes, cucumbers, red onions, olives, feta, garlic, parsley, and dill.

4. Pour the dressing over the salad and toss gently to coat. Taste and adjust seasoning, if needed. Serve immediately.

Note

- You can use Indoor Grilled Chicken (see page 194) for the chicken.

SERVES	PREP	COOK	TOTAL
5	10 minutes	30 minutes	40 minutes

Chianti Chicken Chili

This isn't your average chili. With our precooked ground chicken, this comes together fast and packs so much flavor. Serve it up with some crusty bread or even over some small pasta like ditalini.

2 tablespoons extra-virgin olive oil, plus more for garnish (optional)

1 small white onion, finely chopped

2 celery stalks, finely chopped

1 medium carrot, finely chopped

1 fennel bulb, thinly sliced

6 garlic cloves, minced

½ cup chopped sun-dried tomatoes

½ cup red wine

1x 14.5-ounce (411 g) can fire-roasted tomatoes

1x 15.5-ounce (439 g) can cannellini beans, rinsed and drained

1 cup chicken broth

1 small Parmesan rind (optional)

2 cups cooked ground chicken (see Note)

Salt and freshly ground black pepper, to taste

Grated Pecorino Romano, for garnish (optional)

Basil leaves, for garnish (optional)

1. Heat the oil in a Dutch oven or deep, heavy-bottomed pot set over medium heat. Add the onion, celery, carrot, and fennel. Cook for about 5 minutes until softened.

2. Stir in the garlic and sun-dried tomatoes. Cook for about 5 minutes, until fragrant.

3. Add the wine, stir, and let it simmer for 2 to 3 minutes.

4. Add the fire-roasted tomatoes, beans, broth, and Parmesan rind (if using). Bring to a simmer, about 5 minutes.

5. Stir in the ground chicken and cook for 10 minutes.

6. Remove the rind and discard. Season to taste with salt and pepper. Divide the chili into bowls. Top with Pecorino Romano, basil, and a drizzle of olive oil, if desired.

Note

- You can use Basic Versatile Ground Chicken (see page 192) for the chicken.

SERVES	PREP	COOK	TOTAL
4	10 minutes	50 minutes	1 hour

Sloppy Chicks

Let's make Sloppy Chicks! Think Sloppy Joes but with chicken and Italian vibes. This works great with prepared pulled chicken or even a classic rotisserie. My kids LOVE this one and boy is it simple! This is a great way to use up not only leftover chicken but whatever rolls you have, too.

- 2 tablespoons salted butter
- ½ cup finely diced white onion
- ½ cup finely diced bell pepper
- 2 garlic cloves, minced
- 2 tablespoons tomato paste
- ¾ cup ketchup
- 2 tablespoons honey
- 1 tablespoon apple cider vinegar
- 1 tablespoon Worcestershire sauce
- 1 tablespoon Maggi seasoning sauce (or soy sauce)
- 2 cups shredded chicken (see Note)
- Salt and freshly ground black pepper, to taste
- 4 potato buns, for serving

For serving (optional)

- Pickles
- Sliced onions
- Cheese
- Coleslaw

1. Heat the butter in a large skillet set over medium heat. Add the onion and bell pepper. Cook for 4 to 5 minutes until soft.

2. Stir in the garlic and cook for 30 seconds, until fragrant.

3. Add the tomato paste and cook for about 5 minutes until it darkens.

4. Add the ketchup, honey, apple cider vinegar, Worcestershire, and Maggi. Stir to combine and simmer for 3 to 4 minutes.

5. Stir in the shredded chicken and reduce the heat to low. Simmer for about 5 minutes until the chicken is heated through and well-coated. Season with salt and pepper, to taste.

6. Spoon the pulled chicken mixture generously onto the buns. Top with pickles, onions, cheese, or a scoop of coleslaw, if desired.

Note

- You can use Basic Savory Shredded Chicken (see page 193) for the chicken.

Beef Meal Prep At Work

SERVES	PREP	COOK	TOTAL
6	10 minutes (plus 4 hours or overnight to marinate)	10 to 13 minutes	4 hours 20 minutes

Basic London Broil

London broil gets a bad rap for being tough, but when you treat it right, it's one of the most affordable, flavorful cuts of meat. The trick is using a good marinade, a quick high-heat sear, and letting it rest before slicing against the grain. That's it. And once you've got it, you can enjoy it so many different ways throughout the week.

2 ½ to 3 pounds (1,133 g to 1,360 g) top round steak or London Broil

¼ cup extra-virgin olive oil

¼ cup balsamic vinegar

¼ cup soy sauce

¼ cup honey

1 tablespoon Dijon mustard

4 garlic cloves, minced

4 scallions, minced

Salt and freshly ground black pepper

Special Equipment

Zip-top bag

Cast-iron skillet

Meat thermometer

1. In a large zip-top bag, add the meat, olive oil, vinegar, soy sauce, honey, mustard, garlic, scallions, salt, and pepper. Seal the bag, transfer to the fridge, and allow to marinate for at least 4 hours or up to overnight.

2. Heat a large cast-iron skillet over medium heat for 4 to 5 minutes until it's screaming hot.

3. Remove the steak from the marinade and allow the excess liquid to drip off. Pat it dry.

4. Carefully place the steak in the skillet and cook for 5 to 6 minutes.

5. Flip and cook for 5 to 7 minutes until the meat thermometer reaches 130°F to 135°F (54°C to 57°C) for medium-rare or 135°F to 140°F (57°C to 60°C) for medium.

6. Transfer to a cutting board and cover lightly with foil. Let it rest for 15 minutes before slicing against the grain and serving.

Storage Tips

- Cooked leftovers will last in the fridge for up to 4 days or in the freezer for up to 3 months.

MAKES	PREP	COOK	TOTAL
About 4 cups	5 minutes	20 minutes	25 minutes

Basic Ground Beef

This is the kind of recipe that quietly saves your week. If I'm cooking ground beef, it's probably going to show up three different ways by Friday. That's the beauty of the basics.

1 tablespoon extra-virgin olive oil

1 small white onion, diced

2 garlic cloves, minced

2 pounds (907 g) ground beef

1 tablespoon beef stock

1x 1.1-ounce (31 g) Lipton Recipe Secrets Beefy Onion Soup and Dip Mix

Salt and freshly ground black pepper, to taste

1. Heat the oil in a large frying pan set over medium heat. Add the onion and cook for about 8 minutes until caramelized. Add the garlic and cook for 1 minute.

2. Add the ground beef and cook for about 10 minutes until browned. Drain the meat of excess grease.

3. Return the ground beef back to the pan. Add the beef stock and soup mix and mix well. Season with salt and pepper.

Storage Tips

- Let the meat cool before storing. Divide into zip-top bags and store in the fridge for up to 4 days, or freeze for up to 3 months.

MAKES	PREP	COOK	TOTAL
About 5 cups	15 minutes	3 to 3 ½ hours	4 hours

Basic Braised and Shredded Beef

This is my utility beef. It's tender, juicy, and packed with flavor. But it is also basic enough to go in anything from Italian braised beef sammies to weeknight tacos. You're going to want this one in your back pocket.

3 tablespoons unsalted butter

4 pounds (1,814 g) chuck roast

Salt and freshly ground black pepper

2 teaspoons smoked paprika

1 small yellow onion, sliced

2 celery stalks, thinly sliced

4 garlic cloves, thinly sliced

1 cup beef stock

1 teaspoon apple cider vinegar

1 tablespoon Gravy Master (or Worcestershire sauce)

1 sage leaf

1 rosemary sprig

Special Equipment

Dutch oven

1. Melt the butter in a large Dutch oven or heavy-bottomed pot set over medium heat.

2. Pat the chuck roast dry with paper towels. Season all sides generously with salt, pepper, and smoked paprika.

3. Sear the beef on all sides for 3 to 4 minutes per side, until deep brown. Remove and set aside.

4. Add the sliced onion and celery and cook for 3 to 4 minutes, scraping up the brown bits. Add the garlic and cook for 1 minute until fragrant.

5. Add the meat, beef stock, apple cider vinegar, Gravy Master, sage, and rosemary.

6. Cover tightly and reduce heat to low. Let it simmer gently for 3 to 3½ hours, turning once or twice, until the meat is fork-tender and falling apart.

7. Once the beef is tender, shred with two forks and return to the pot to soak up the juices. Taste and adjust seasoning as needed.

Storage Tips

- Store the cooked meat in the braising liquid in the fridge for up to 5 days or freeze for up to 3 months.

SERVES	PREP	COOK	TOTAL
5	15 minutes	35 minutes	50 minutes

Faux Bolognese Stuffed Shells

This one is very Italian-American of me! Stuffed shells are the kind of dish that feels fancy but are secretly very forgiving. This version combines pre-cooked ground beef and some other fridge staples to make a really satisfying filling. Top with marinara (homemade or jarred!) and mozzarella. Bake until nice and bubbly and you have comfort food at its finest! Serve with a nice green salad.

- 20–25 jumbo pasta shells
- 2 tablespoons extra-virgin olive oil, divided
- 2 cups cooked Basic Ground Beef (see page 213)
- 1 cup ricotta
- 1 cup grated Pecorino Romano
- 1 tablespoon Calabrian chili paste
- 1 large egg
- 2 garlic cloves, minced
- 1 tablespoon chopped basil
- Salt and freshly ground black pepper, to taste
- 2 cups marinara sauce, divided
- 1 cup shredded mozzarella
- Chopped parsley, for garnish

Special Equipment

Baking dish

Zip-top bag

1. Preheat the oven to 400°F (200°C).

2. Bring a large pot of salted water to a boil. Cook the shells until just shy of al dente. Drain and cool slightly. Drizzle with 1 tablespoon of olive oil to prevent sticking.

3. In a large bowl, add the cooked ground beef, ricotta, Pecorino Romano, Calabrian chili paste, egg, garlic, basil, salt, and pepper. Mix until combined. Transfer the mixture to a large zip-top bag. Set aside.

4. In the bottom of a baking dish, add half of the marinara sauce and spread in an even layer.

5. Snip a small corner from the top of the bag and pipe it into the shells. Place the shells seam side-up in the baking dish.

6. Pour the remaining marinara over the shells. Cover with shredded mozzarella. Cover loosely with foil. Bake for 20 minutes. Remove the foil and bake for an additional 5 minutes until the cheese is melted and bubbly.

7. Garnish with parsley.

SERVES	PREP	COOK	TOTAL
4	10 minutes	1 hour 15 minutes	1 hour 25 minutes

Potato Cheesesteak Melts

This recipe is a hearty, satisfying twist on one of my favorite sandwiches. It's a great way to repurpose leftover ground beef while skipping the bread, which to me just feels more like "dinner." It's perfect for a cozy weeknight meal. Don't be scared to get creative with your toppings.

4 large russet potatoes, washed thoroughly and pricked with a fork

2 tablespoons extra-virgin olive oil

Salt and freshly ground black pepper, to taste

2 tablespoons salted butter, plus more for serving

1 medium yellow onion, thinly sliced

1 bell pepper, thinly sliced

1½ cups cooked Basic Ground Beef (see page 213)

1 tablespoon steak sauce, such as Peter Luger

2 garlic cloves, minced

4 slices of provolone

Pickled cherry peppers, for garnish (optional)

Pickles, chopped, for garnish (optional)

Sautéed mushrooms, for garnish (optional)

1. Preheat the oven to 400°F (200°C).

2. Rub the potatoes with the olive oil and sprinkle with salt. Bake on the oven rack for 55 to 60 minutes until fork-tender and crispy.

3. Melt the butter in a large skillet set over medium heat. Add the onions and bell pepper. Cook for about 12 minutes until caramelized.

4. Add the ground beef, steak sauce, garlic, salt, and pepper. Cook for 3 to 5 minutes.

5. Top with the provolone. Cover, remove from the heat, and let sit.

6. Fluff the inside of the cooked potatoes with a fork. Add butter and salt to taste. Top with the beef mixture, followed by the pickled cherry peppers, pickles, and mushrooms, if desired.

SERVES	PREP	COOK	TOTAL
4	5 minutes	25 minutes	30 minutes

Eggs alla Nonna

Every time I make meatballs, you know there will be leftovers. Now, the obvious meal idea would be meatball parm heroes, baked ziti, or even my Meatball and Vegetable Stew (see page 45)! But let's think out of the box! Let's make Eggs alla Nonna! This all comes together so quickly, which makes for a perfect weeknight meal.

1 tablespoon extra-virgin olive oil

2 anchovy fillets

3 cups Marinara Sauce (see page 43)

8 cooked Classic Meatballs (see page 43), cut into bite-size pieces

8 large eggs

Salt and freshly ground black pepper, to taste

Crushed red pepper flakes (optional)

For serving

1 tablespoon chopped basil

1 tablespoon chopped parsley

4 tablespoons ricotta

Grated Pecorino Romano

Semi-Semolina Loaf (see page 158)

1. Heat the oil in a large skillet set over medium heat. Add the anchovy filets and cook for 1 to 2 minutes.

2. Add the marinara sauce and bring to a gentle simmer, about 5 minutes.

3. Add the meatballs. Cover and cook for about 8 minutes, stirring occasionally.

4. Use the back of a spoon to create 8 small wells in the sauce. Crack an egg into each well.

5. Reduce the heat to low. Cover and cook for 6 to 8 minutes until the whites are set but yolks are still soft.

6. Season with salt, pepper, and red pepper flakes (if using). Top with basil, parsley, ricotta, and Pecorino Romano. Serve immediately with slices of warm Semi-Semolina Loaf (see page 158) for dipping.

SERVES	PREP	COOK	TOTAL
4	10 minutes	50 minutes	1 hour

Arancini-Stuffed Peppers

Arancini-Stuffed Peppers sounds wild, right? You get all the delicious flavors of the rice ball without the frying! This is a great way to use your leftover rice and ground beef. These also can be used for other meals, so make a few extra to freeze.

3 bell peppers, ribs and seeds removed, halved

4 tablespoons extra-virgin olive oil, divided

Salt and freshly ground black pepper, to taste

1 small white onion, diced

3 garlic cloves, minced

2 tablespoons tomato paste

1 teaspoon granulated sugar

1½ cups cooked rice

1½ cups cooked Basic Ground Beef (see page 213)

¼ cup frozen peas

1 large egg

½ cup shredded mozzarella

¼ cup grated Pecorino Romano

2 tablespoons chopped parsley

½ cup Italian-seasoned breadcrumbs

Special Equipment

9 x 13-inch (23 x 33 cm) baking dish

1. Preheat the oven to 400°F (200°C).

2. Rub the bell peppers with 1 tablespoon olive oil. Season with salt and pepper. Place them in a baking dish, cut side down. Bake for 8 minutes to soften.

3. Heat 2 tablespoons of olive oil in a saucepan over medium heat. Add the onion and garlic, and cook for about 8 minutes until fragrant.

4. Add the tomato paste and sugar and cook for about 3 minutes until it darkens a little bit. Remove from the heat.

5. In a large bowl, add the cooked rice, beef, peas, egg, mozzarella, Pecorino Romano, parsley, and the tomato-onion mixture. Season to taste with salt and pepper. Stir.

6. Divide the mixture between the roasted peppers. Sprinkle the breadcrumbs on top. Drizzle with the remaining olive oil.

7. Bake, covered, for 20 minutes. Then increase the oven temperature to 450°F (230°C) and bake for 8 more minutes.

8. Serve and enjoy!

MAKES	PREP	COOK	TOTAL
12 bites	10 minutes (plus thawing time for the pastry)	40 minutes	50 minutes

Open-Faced Beef and Brie Bites

Leftover steak calls for beef and Brie bites. It seems very bougie but really, it's just a great use of leftovers and condiments sitting in your fridge!

Cooking spray

1 tablespoon salted butter

1 small red onion, thinly sliced

2 garlic cloves, minced

1x 17.3-ounce (490 g) box puff pastry sheets, thawed

Flour, for work surface

3 tablespoons Dijon mustard

1 tablespoon honey

1 tablespoon mayonnaise

1 teaspoon chopped thyme

1½ cups Basic London Broil (see page 212), diced

1x 8-ounce (227 g) Brie wheel, diced

Balsamic glaze, for serving

Special Equipment

2 Jumbo muffin tins

Pastry brush

1. Preheat the oven to 375°F (190°C). Grease two jumbo muffin tins with cooking spray.

2. Melt the butter in a small skillet set over medium heat. Add the onion and cook for about 15 minutes until caramelized.

3. Add the garlic and cook for 1 minute. Remove from heat.

4. Roll out the thawed puff pastry on a lightly floured surface. Cut each sheet into 6 equal squares (about 3 inches (7.5 cm) each). Transfer the puff pastry squares to the muffin tins and fit the dough in each cavity.

5. In a small bowl, whisk together the mustard, honey, mayonnaise, and thyme.

6. Brush the inside of each piece of pastry with the honey-mustard mixture.

7. Evenly distribute the caramelized onions, beef, and Brie between the 12 cups.

8. Bake for 20 to 22 minutes. Cool slightly before serving with a drizzle of balsamic glaze.

SERVES	PREP	COOK	TOTAL
6	15 minutes	30 minutes	45 minutes

Reinvented Hamburger Helper

This next one is a twist on a childhood classic, Hamburger Helper. My mom never bought packaged items so I would go to my friends' houses and get so excited to see they were having Hamburger Helper for dinner. I would go home and share with my mom; she would try to recreate the flavors, but it always just tasted Italian. DELICIOUS! But not Hamburger Helper. My version is giving American classic vibes and even my kids love it!

1 pound (454 g) medium shells

2 tablespoons salted butter

1 medium shallot, finely diced

½ red bell pepper, diced (about ¼ cup)

2 tablespoons all-purpose flour

2 cups half-and-half

2 cups cooked Basic Ground Beef (see page 213)

1 tablespoon chicken bouillon powder

1 teaspoon ground nutmeg

1 teaspoon Dijon mustard

Freshly ground black pepper, to taste

1 cup shredded Fontina

1 cup shredded Havarti

1. Bring a large pot of water to a boil. Cook the shells just shy of al dente. Drain.

2. Melt the butter in a large saucepan set over medium heat. Add the shallots and peppers. Cook for 3 to 5 minutes until tender.

3. Build your roux by adding in the flour and cook, about 3 minutes.

4. Slowly whisk in the half-and-half until fully combined. Add the ground beef, chicken bouillon powder, nutmeg, mustard, and black pepper. Whisk thoroughly.

5. Reduce the heat. Add the Fontina and Havarti, one handful in at a time, whisking in between each addition.

6. Add the cooked shells and stir. Cook for 3 to 5 minutes until you reach your desired consistency.

SERVES	PREP	TOTAL
4	10 minutes	15 minutes

Caprese Couscous

Protein and grain bowls are huge right now. How many times during the week do you have leftovers of each? The next night, pair them together, add a ton of fun toppings, and BOOM! It feels like a completely different meal. Here is my favorite combination but use what you have on hand.

4 tablespoons extra-virgin olive oil, divided

½ cup slivered almonds

Juice of 2 lemons

1 teaspoon maple syrup

Salt and freshly ground black pepper, to taste

2 cups cooked Israeli couscous (bonus points if it's the Lemon Herby Couscous on page 119)

1 cup arugula

½ cup chopped sun-dried peppers

½ cup chopped Castelvetrano olives

½ cup quartered cherry tomatoes

1 celery stalk, diced

1½ cups Basic London Broil (see page 212), cubed

1 cup quartered cigliene mozzarella

10 basil leaves, torn

Special Equipment

Mason jar

1. Heat 1 tablespoon oil in a medium skillet set over medium heat. Add the almonds and toast for 2 to 3 minutes, stirring frequently until lightly golden. Remove from heat. Cool.

2. In a mason jar, add the lemon juice, the remaining 3 tablespoons olive oil, maple syrup, salt, and pepper. Seal with the lid and shake until well combined. Set aside.

3. In a large mixing bowl, add the couscous, arugula, sun-dried peppers, olives, cherry tomatoes, celery, and toasted almonds. Toss to combine.

4. Add the cubed beef and mozzarella and gently toss, being careful not to mash the cheese too much. Season to taste with salt and pepper.

5. Add the basil to the dressing. Pour over the salad and toss to combine. Serve at room temperature.

SERVES	PREP	COOK	TOTAL
4	10 minutes	10 minutes	20 minutes

Beef and Roasted Vegetable Panini

We do sheet pan dinners around here often. Some sort of protein and vegetable, normally marinated in a balsamic vinegar mixture. The leftovers make for killer beef and vegetable paninis. And no, you don't need a panini press to make these!

2 tablespoons mayonnaise

1 tablespoon prepared horseradish

1 garlic clove, grated

4 ciabatta rolls

8 slices of havarti

2 cups thinly sliced leftover steak (bonus points if it's the Basic London Broil on page 212)

1 cup leftover roasted vegetables

Special Equipment

Cast-iron skillet or grill pan

Heavy weight or cast-iron press

1. In a small bowl, add the mayonnaise, horseradish, and garlic. Mix well. Set aside.

2. Slice each ciabatta roll in half and spread a generous layer of the horseradish mayonnaise on both halves.

3. On the bottom half of each roll, add 1 slice of havarti, followed by the sliced steak.

4. Pile on the roasted vegetables and the remaining havarti. Top with the other half of the roll.

5. Heat a frying pan, cast-iron skillet, or grill pan over medium heat. Place the sandwiches in the pan and place a heavy, heatproof object like a cast-iron skillet or another heavy pan on top.

6. Toast for 3 to 4 minutes. Flip, press, and cook for 3 to 4 minutes until the bread is toasted and the cheese is melted.

7. Slice the paninis diagonally and serve warm.

SERVES	PREP	COOK	TOTAL
6	10 minutes	20 minutes	30 minutes

Eggplant and Beef Lasagna

A lasagna without pasta may sound unusual but using grilled or fried eggplant (or zucchini) as a substitute for traditional sheets creates a flavorful, lower-carb alternative. Layered with leftover shredded beef, this dish offers the same comforting qualities of classic lasagna with a lighter twist.

1 cup ricotta

1 large egg

1 tablespoon chopped fresh mint or basil

½ cup grated Pecorino Romano

Salt and freshly ground black pepper, to taste

2 tablespoons extra-virgin olive oil, divided

12 sheets of fried or grilled eggplant (or 24 slices of zucchini)

1 cup cooked Basic Ground Beef (see page 213)

1 cup Marinara Sauce, (recipe on page 43, jarred works fine too)

1 cup shredded mozzarella

Special Equipment

9 x 13-inch (23 x 33 cm) baking dish (2.5 inches/6.5 cm deep)

Pastry brush

1. Preheat the oven to 375°F (190°C).

2. In a large bowl, add the ricotta, egg, mint (or basil), and Pecorino Romano. Mix. Season to taste with salt and pepper.

3. Lightly brush the bottom of a 9 x 13-inch (23 x 33 cm) baking dish with 1 tablespoon olive oil.

4. Layer the eggplant slices on the bottom of the baking dish. Spread a layer of ricotta mixture on top of the eggplant, followed by a layer of the beef, marinara sauce, and mozzarella. Repeat layers until all ingredients are used, finishing with mozzarella on top.

5. Drizzle the remaining olive oil over the lasagna.

6. Bake for 20 minutes, uncovered, or until the cheese is bubbly and golden.

7. Let rest 5 minutes before serving.

AND
THAT'S
DINNER!

Acknowledgments

First and foremost, to all of you! None of this would be possible without each one of you reading this book. All the support and love that you show me and my content daily is what keeps my creativity thriving. You have all made this journey so special and I'm forever grateful.

To my incredible husband Tom, thank you for your endless patience and your constant taste testing. You've been my biggest supporter for as long as I can remember, in and out of the kitchen. Thank you for holding it down in our home while allowing time for me to achieve my goals—we really are a team.

To my two daughters Serafina and Mariella, may you always find love in our kitchen and laughter at our table. May you grow up knowing food isn't just about recipes; it's about love and making memories in the kitchen. Mom loves you always.

To my mom, there are never enough words to express my gratitude. I remember you working tirelessly my whole childhood, holding down multiple jobs just to keep a roof over our head and food on the table. I also remember us spending time in the kitchen together, making all that stuff just disappear. This book is as much yours as it is mine. I hope I've made you and Grandma proud.

To my managers Cameron and Evita and all my family, thank you for always having my best interest at heart. Your belief in me has helped make this dream a reality. I hope you know I am so appreciative of your guidance and support.

Index

R

S

About the Author

Born and raised in Queens, New York, Leah Victoria has always had a passion for good food and accessible recipes. Before becoming a content creator and stay-at-home mom, Leah worked in catering and honed her culinary skills as the owner of Leah's Italian Apples, a pop-up business specializing in arancini. She entertains online with tried-and-true recipes, time-saving hacks, and a no-nonsense vibe that invites everyone to the table. She lives in New Jersey with her husband and two daughters.